Praise for FOUNDATIONS OF TAPPING

"In an increasingly challenging world it is a gift to find a book like **'Foundations of Tapping'** *by Stacey Webb. Stacey shares with us her knowledge of tapping in a way that encourages us to make this a daily part of our life. She is a caring and compassionate writer and her latest book gives us a tool to meet our daily challenges more comfortably. Tapping as shown in* **'Foundations of Tapping'** *is easy to learn and is a valuable resource to buffer us in times of need. You will be glad to have this knowledge"*

Angelique Adams – Soul Mentor, Intuitive Intelligence Tapping

"Stacey Webb has poured her heart and soul into this must-have bundle! I couldn't wait to turn every page as I learned something new that will benefit me as I advance through life. These techniques will become part of your toolkit in life because life happens to us at all times and when we know how to recover from it with the right tools and resources, we don't fall too far. I highly recommend **Foundations of Tapping** *and its* **Companion Workbook** *to everyone reading this and your loved ones."*

Karen Mc Dermott – Publisher, Author, and Life Philosopher

Once you have read **'Foundations of Tapping'**, *you will keep the book close by as a reference. Stacey Webb*

has packed the pages (and the **Companion Workbook**) full of simple tools and advice, ready for readers of all ages to put into practise. Stacey has done a wonderful job turning this alternative form of therapy into something comforting and familiar. I found myself tapping along as I was reading, feeling noticeably more calmer after completing the exercises. **'Foundations of Tapping'** will benefit anyone who wants to bring a sense of calm into their life, but will be especially useful for those seeking relief from anxiety, phobias, PTSD or any form of healing. The author has credibility and experience, having successfully achieved fabulous results utilising various methods of tapping in both her work and personal life. **'Foundations of Tapping'** is sure to have a positive impact on your life, as it has on mine. I would highly recommend this book for beginners, as well as those who want to expand the knowledge they already have of tapping.

Lisa Benson – Author of *'Where Have I Been All My Life?'*

Stacey Webb's, **'Foundations of Tapping'** along with her beautifully presented **'Foundations of Tapping Companion Workbook'** came into my life at exactly the right moment, where I was looking for something to assist me and my nervous system. As a mental health worker, I understand the importance of self care and not burning out, and so am always on the look out for tools and life practices that can assist me in supporting my nervous system. Along with being kind to myself and *aiming to live a peaceful life. In the **Foundations of Tapping**, Stacey gifts the reader with so many tools and opportunities along with easy practices to help you maintain daily, beneficial tapping that can help you heal on so many levels. I highly recommend these insightful books packed with Stacey's gift of knowledge on tapping and all the phenomenal benefits it can bring to your life, and those around you. Congratulations Stacey Webb, and Thank You.*

Mickey Martin – Award Winning Author

"The best self-help books make you feel like the author is sitting beside you, guiding you through the practices suggested in their books. Ms. Webb's book is no exception. As you read, you can almost hear her calm voice leading you through the exercises, creating a safe space in which to learn, and to move at one's pace. This book and it's accompanying workbook create a relationship between the author and the reader. One that encourages a sense of tranquility and trust whilst applying the practical advice."

D.D. Line – Author

"Very informative and loved the practices in the workbook! Tapping is something my children and I use often, on ourselves, each other, and our animals."

Kia West – Spiritual Director

"I am enamoured by the bundle that Stacey Webb has created. Not only do you get the why, but the how.

With many opportunities along the way to expand your toolkit in simple, accessible, and immediate ways. The addition of the **'Foundations of Tapping Companion Workbook'** *is a panacea for my heart as someone that loves to journal and track the experiment that is life. Having all the prompts ready for my 30 day practice, which I just fill in is a massive timesaver and consistent way to build a flexible and dynamic daily practice. I wholeheartedly recommend* **'Foundations of Tapping'** *and the* **'Foundations of Tapping Companion Workbook'** *to all my family and friends. In a world that is saturated with fluff, this is a welcome balm of practical wisdom and lived experience that will fit into any lifestyle and circumstance.*

Alison Haitana – Author, Story Alchemist, and Tech Mystic

FOUNDATIONS OF TAPPING

Inviting EFT and Other Tapping Practices into Your Life

Reconnecting to your innate tools for your healing journey

STACEY WEBB

Copyright © 2023 by Stacey Webb

First published in Australia in 2023 by Stacey Webb

All rights reserved. No part of this book may be reproduced by any mechanical, photographic, or electronic process, or in the form of phonographic recording; nor may it be stored in a retrieval system, transmitted, or otherwise be copied for public or private use - other than for "fair use" as brief quotations embodied in articles and reviews – without prior written permission from the publisher.

The author of this book does not dispense medical advice or prescribe the use of any technique as a form of treatment for physical, emotional, or medical problems without the advice of a physician, either directly or indirectly. The intent of the author is only to offer information of a general nature to help you in your quest for emotional and spiritual well-being. In the event you use any of the information in this book for yourself, the author and publisher assume no responsibility for your actions.

Because of the dynamic nature of the Internet, any web addresses or links contained in this book may have changed since publication and may no longer be valid.

Cover design by Ida Jensson

Edited by Dannielle Line

All images by Rachael Cannard

ISBN: 978-0-6458119-0-2 (Paperback)

ISBN: 978-0-6458119-1-9 (Ebook)

I dedicate this book to you, dear reader. For picking up this book with curiosity and willingness as you walk the path of your healing journey. It is my privilege to take this journey with you.

Acknowledgment of Country

As I explore the divine lands of Colomatta and its surroundings, I feel its expansive nature. In those moments and in every moment in between I acknowledge the Dharug and Gundungurra people of the Ngurra Nation as the infinite custodians of this place. I acknowledge your custodial care has been integral to the wonderful expression of this magical place. I see that the nurturing, care and healing you provide to this land flows back to the people through the elements of this place. I stand and witness the deep and sacred spiritual connection you have to all those elements of this Country. I pay deep respects to the Elders with much gratitude for the powerful way they lead the community. I am committed to being an ally to the Aboriginal community and supporting Aboriginal-led movements toward an equitable society.

Author Note

Emotional Freedom Techniques are still considered experimental in nature. Although it is gaining scientific support; it is not yet widely accepted as a formally validated scientific technique. It is important you take full responsibility for your own health. The content provided in this workbook is not a substitute for traditional medical attention, counselling, therapy, or advice from a qualified healthcare practitioner. It is not intended to be used to treat, diagnose, cure, or prevent any disease or disorder.

Table of Contents

Welcome	XV
1. The Foundations	1
2. The Basic Recipe	20
3. Tapping through the Layers	51
4. Personal Peace Procedure	65
5. Chakra Tapping	74
6. Other Tapping Practices	91
7. Inviting Tapping into Your Life	101
8. Tapping Scripts	107
9. Reflection	151
Endnotes	153
Thank You	155
Resources	156
Letter of Gratitude	157
About the Author	159

Welcome

Hello and welcome, my friend. I am so happy you have chosen to read *Foundations of Tapping: Inviting EFT and Other Tapping Practices into Your Life.* This book is a true reconnection to your innate tools for your healing journey and I am honoured to share this information with you.

My name is Stacey Webb. I am an Intuitive Somatic Mentor, Trauma-Trained Somatic Practitioner, a Warrior of Grace, and a Multi-Award-Winning Author.

I wrote this book and created the accompanying workbook, *Foundations of Tapping Companion Workbook*, as I wish it was something I had when I was learning to incorporate tapping into my own healing journey. I have spent seventeen years as a police officer, predominantly in criminal investigation, where I was surrounded by people experiencing trauma in varying states. Whilst still achieving my job in investigation, I wanted to best support them and their nervous system. I started learning about the nervous system which led me to learning about Emotional Freedom Techniques (EFT) and other forms of tapping. When I used tapping with members of the public and colleagues to support their nervous system, I noticed how much I needed tapping myself. That I, too, was stuck in patterns, limiting myself, doubting myself, stressed, overwhelmed, and experiencing fear and trauma. Tapping has supported my nervous system, transforming my life, and I now use it every day. In fact, I love tapping so much, I became an EFT Practitioner and Intuitive Intelligence Tapping Practitioner.

    Now, as an Intuitive Somatic Mentor, I include tapping in my work as a Somatic Practitioner, supporting people experiencing trauma through a somatic lens. I create and hold space for people. I witness them as a whole, along with the energetic, physical, emotional, mental, and spiritual shifts they may experience during our sessions. People process deeply rooted patterns of pain and limitation. I've seen them create safety within their body and their nervous system, cultivating a relationship with themselves as they release through the layers of their own healing journey. I've seen my clients embody a lightness they've not felt in years as they reconnect with their heart, their inner child, and their intuition.

    Most of us are living a life filled with high stress surrounded in a trauma culture. We place so much pressure on ourselves, put limitations on ourselves, and hide our true feelings, which may include resentment, anger, shame, and guilt. This can leave us feeling alone and isolated, as though we are never good enough, never worthy enough, always a failure, and maybe even more.

    Does this sound familiar to you?

FOUNDATIONS OF TAPPING

It is possible that deep down, this may resonate with you if you have chosen to read this book.

I want you to know it's possible to release emotions stuck within. It is possible to change these patterns and let go of the stress, the doubt, the anxiety, the fear, and the trauma, transforming these limiting energies into something lighter and expansive within your nervous system.

I created this book and *Foundations of Tapping Companion Workbook* to empower you in your own transformation. To have this tool in your hands to help you let go of the things holding you back.

I also want you to know this isn't really about the tool at all. As much as I'm providing you with information about EFT and other forms of tapping, I want you to understand the true magic of tapping is not the tapping itself. It is our ability to safely acknowledge, process, and release the attachments to the things we are finding difficult and challenging. We are used to pushing our feelings down, avoiding them, deflecting them. To save face and show how we can do it all. Not wanting to reveal our true feelings or true motivations even though we know doing that can make it hard to process some of the heavier things we are experiencing in life.

It's important to incorporate all aspects of the physical, mental, emotional, and spiritual parts of yourself and to make sure you are constantly checking in, connecting, acknowledging, validating, and witnessing yourself as you feel your feelings. Feeling uncomfortable and showing vulnerability can be challenging and scary. However, you have strength and courage within, even if you don't believe it right now. Just picking up this book shows you possess these qualities. I promise you it is worth it because on the other side of all that discomfort and all that pain is something truly magical.

This book has an accompanying book called *Foundations of Tapping Companion Workbook*. I recommend having both books together because they support and complement each other. To ensure a smooth transition between them, the chapters in both books are the same. You can purchase the *Companion Workbook* at the same place you purchased this book. You can also purchase a PDF version of the *Companion Workbook* from my website at www.staceywebb.com.au under the Books tab.

This book contains the history, philosophy, and principles of Emotional Freedom Techniques and other tapping practices. By reading and participating in the practices, you will learn how to use the Basic Recipe, Personal Peace Procedure, Chakra Tapping, and ways to incorporate tapping every day to support your healing journey. Having the *Companion Workbook* will allow you to participate in the deeper practices of tapping mentioned in this book to support your healing journey.

Allow yourself to flow at a pace that feels comfortable for you. Give yourself permission to interact, to join in the practices, and integrate the learnings. You might be surprised at what you learn.

CHAPTER ONE

The Foundations

REMINDER

This book has an accompanying book called **Foundations of Tapping Companion Workbook.** *I recommend having both books together because they support and compliment each other. You can purchase the* **Foundations of Tapping Companion Workbook** *at the same place you purchased this book. You can also purchase a PDF version of the* **Foundations of Tapping Companion Workbook** *from my website at www.staceywebb.com.au under the Books tab.*

What is EFT?

EFT, otherwise known as Emotional Freedom Techniques or tapping, is an energy-based field of psychology that combines eastern energy meridian knowledge with western psychology. EFT draws on the same system of energy pathways that have been utilised in acupuncture for thousands of years to address both physical and emotional issues. EFT is also acupuncture without needles and is a form of acupressure.

EFT is safe and easy to use, and it brings freedom from uncomfortable emotions. As you gently tap with your fingertips on these meridian points, you say some statements that verbalise the problem, followed by a generalised affirmation phrase. The reason we repeat these phrases while tapping on the meridian points is to balance the energy system within your body, releasing any psychological stress, fear, and trauma.

With tapping, you can transform negative behaviours into empowering ones. Allowing you to be more mindful and intentional with your decisions.

What can you use EFT for?

We can use EFT for pretty much anything and everything. The meta-analysis evaluating the effect of EFT treatment for anxiety, depression, phobias, and posttraumatic stress disorder (PTSD). Or as I prefer to call it, posttraumatic stress injury (PTSI) has found it to be 'moderate' to 'large' revealing EFT to be a stable and mature method with an extensive evidence base. Its use in primary care settings as a safe, rapid, reliable, and effective treatment for both psychological and medical diagnosis continues to grow.[1]

With EFT, you can rekindle a connection with your emotions, even if you previously felt disconnected from them. The beauty of this technique is it is both quick and efficient, and you don't have to revisit every traumatic experience to experience relief because of EFT's cumulative effect. Meaning once you have completed working on an issue or event it is likely that many similar issues will lose their charge, power, and effect.

Everyone can benefit from tapping. If you have a problem, there's a good chance you can tap on it.

History of EFT

EFT was developed by Gary Craig in the US, an engineer and performance coach. He trained with Dr. Roger Callahan in Thought Field Therapy (TFT), where you use tapping on specific energy points in certain sequences to restore an individual's health and wellness. This is a more complex form of tapping. Gary Craig simplified the TFT method, turning it into an easily available technique that would cover all the body's meridians at once. This made it so much more accessible for everyone to learn and use.

There is extensive scientific research linking EFT to epigenetics, neuroplasticity, memory reconsolidation, stress release, and psychoneuroimmunology. This research shows how our electromagnetic energy system is intimately connected, carrying information throughout our bodies, and the many benefits EFT can provide in your life and health.

How does EFT work?

The limbic system, a part of our brain, plays a key role in managing emotions and memories. This system contains the amygdala and hippocampus, with the amygdala specifically responsible for processing fear-related emotions and memories.

To understand the power of the amygdala, think of it as our body's smoke detector[2], sensing smoke or fire. It senses and notifies you when it believes something is threatening your safety. The amygdala signals the brain to mobilise the body for a fight-or-flight response.

Now think of the amygdala as having its own auto-correction mechanism. If it has been programmed with a trauma response from past experiences, it may react to similar triggers in the future, even if they are not actually threatening. The amygdala does not differentiate between real and perceived threats.

Imagine you are in primary school, and you put your

hand up to answer a question. However, your answer doesn't match the question. You hear a student in class laughing and you believe they are laughing at you. Such incidents can cause the mind-body connection to associate speaking in front of people, self-expression, and other related actions with danger. This can cause the amygdala to activate in response to similar situations or even the anticipation of similar experiences.

The hippocampus is another part of the limbic system that controls contextual associations. Its role is to save memories of events in our lives.

Our Amygdala perceives a threat and sounds the alarm. The hippocampus tells the body to act, and the body reacts by going into fight/ flight/ freeze/ fawn (trauma responses) in anticipation of the perceived threat.

When the amygdala is relaxed, no signal is sent, so your hippocampus doesn't tell your body to respond.

The amazing thing about EFT is that it sends a calming response to the amygdala. Tapping on the meridian endpoints turns off the amygdala's alarm, deactivating the brain's arousal pathways.

When EFT is applied to a stressful event, fear, or trauma, the amygdala does not set off the alarm. Instead, it allows you to remain calm.

Tapping while experiencing or even discussing a stressful event counteracts its impact and reprograms the hippocampus[3], which evaluates current signals against past threats and informs the amygdala whether a present signal represents a genuine threat. It also allows us to tap into a traumatic event without having to tell the story of the memory. This is because the negative charge from intense emotional events is stored in our bodies and EFT helps in releasing them.

All that change in the brain's chemistry enables emotional and psychological shifts within your psyche, and you can see and feel things from a different perspective.

Tapping and Energetics

The EFT Discovery statement by Gary Craig is, 'The cause of ALL negative emotions is a disruption in the body's energy system.'[4]

What does that mean?

Everything is energy. That includes us. In our energy system, our body has a constant flow of energy that connects to all the meridian points. When we become unbalanced within our body, the flow of energy starts to short circuits and can create a 'zzzzt'.

What Gary Craig's discovery statement means is that the thought (distressing memory) causes your energy system to become disrupted. This creates a 'zzzzt', a short circuit within the energy system. When energy flows freely, there are no short circuits, or 'zzzzts' within the energy system.

If the 'zzzzt' doesn't occur, then a negative emotion

isn't experienced. This is why some people are affected by certain memories because their energy system becomes unbalanced when thinking about those memories while others don't. If the memory does not disrupt the body's energy system, then the negative emotion cannot occur.

We can effectively give support to the emotion by going straight to the energy system. By tapping on the energy system, acknowledging it, and balancing it while you are tuned into the thought, the emotion doesn't occur. This is why EFT is great to use for trauma. You do not have to speak about the trauma as you tune into it for EFT to support you and be effective in its work.

Benefits of EFT

One of the best things about tapping is it is so simple. It feels downright miraculous sometimes to have access to something so transformative right at your fingertips. Research has shown some of the benefits of EFT: [5]

- Lowers your cortisol levels.

- Lowers anxiety.

- Lowers depression.

- Lowers blood pressure.

- Lowers pain.

- Lowers PTSI symptoms.
- Lowers food cravings.
- Increases immune system markers.
- Increases happiness.
- Increases confidence and self-esteem.

Other benefits of using the EFT include the following:
- It is simple and painless.
- It is easy to learn.
- You can do it by yourself.
- It is less time-consuming.
- It can be used with specific emotional intent toward your unique life challenges.
- It gives you the power to heal yourself.
- It drastically reduces distress that gives rise to problems, and
- Enhances performance.

How would your life look if you could shift the needle on any one of these markers?

It could look very different, and it is amazing how

quickly and easily we can shift all these things with tapping.

Common signs you may experience with EFT

You may experience some things during or after tapping. Some common signs showing tapping is repairing energy disruptions in your body are:
- Gasping (an exhale of surprise).
- Sighing (an inhale of relief).
- Yawning (this is a big sign to show energy is shifting!).
- Burping.
- Farting.
- Tears or watery eyes.
- Coughing.
- Lump in the throat clearing.
- A knot in the chest clearing.
- A buzzing feeling through the body, (as if more oxygen is flowing all over).
- Tension/ heaviness easing in parts of your body.

- Breath becomes slow and deep.
- Feeling tired.
- Pain relief in a body part when you were not even targeting that pain.
- A felt sense within the body.
- A feeling of safety within your body.

Tapping Points

This process is simple to learn and can be self-applied. It is also powerful, as it works to directly shift energy.

Tapping is done with the first two fingers (the pointer and middle) of each hand. For each of these points, you can use one hand or both hands at the same time, and/or you can alternate your hands. Do whatever feels comfortable for you.

Main Tapping Points

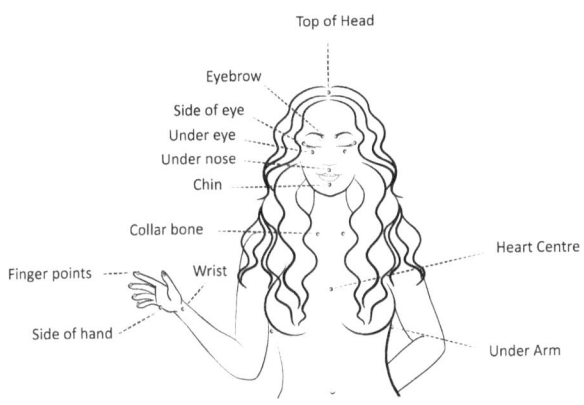

These tapping points are considered the main tapping points. When you tap on these points in sequence, it is considered tapping a 'round'.

Side of Hand (SoH). This point, used during the 'set up statement' is located on the side of your hand, the soft fleshy part between the base of the baby finger and the wrist. Tapping on the side of the hand facilitates the release of resistance to change, letting go, feelings of vulnerability, worry, and obsessions. Tapping on this point supports relaxation of the nervous system, healing from grief, finding joy, and enhancing connection to the present moment, while letting go of what no longer serves you.

Eyebrow (EB) begins at the top of the nose to the beginning of the eyebrow. Tapping on the eyebrow releases trauma, hurt, sadness, restlessness, frustration, impatience, and dread. It also encourages emotional healing, allowing for clearer thinking and a feeling of peace within.

Side of Eye (SE) is located at the end of the eyebrow beside the corner of the eye, just below the temple on the bone. Tapping on the eyebrow can help alleviate trauma, pain, sadness, agitation, frustration, impatience, and dread. This tapping point supports emotional healing, leading to a clearer mind, and a sense of inner peace.

Under Eye (UE) is located directly under the eye on the bone. Tapping under the eye can help release fear, anxiety, anxiety, worry, nervousness, disappointment, and feelings of emptiness. This tapping point supports feelings of contentment, serenity, and safety within the nervous system.

Under Nose (UN) is located between the nose and upper lip. Tapping under the nose can help alleviate embarrassment, a lack of control, shame, guilt, grief, fear of failure, and ridicule. It also helps regulate the nervous system and supports self-acceptance, self-empowerment, and a heightened sense of self-awareness and compassion for oneself and others.

Chin Point (CP) is located between the lower lip and the chin in the depression under the mouth. Tapping on the chin can help alleviate confusion, shame, embarrassment, and self-doubt. This tapping point supports clarity, confidence, self-assurance, and self-acceptance.

Collarbone (CB) is located one inch below the

collarbone notch and one inch out from the collarbone towards the shoulders. In the middle of the V within the fleshy part. Tapping on the collarbone can help release fear, feelings of being trapped, indecision, worry, and stress. This tapping point supports a sense of forward movement, confidence, and clarity.

Underarm (UA) is located about ten centimetres/four inches below the armpit. In the middle of the bra strap is located if you wear one. Tapping under the arm can help alleviate guilt, worry, hopelessness, insecurity, and low self-esteem. Tapping on this point supports clarity, confidence, calmness, and a sense of compassion for oneself and others.

There are two ways you can tap on the underarm point. One way is to have your hand cross the front of your body and tap under your arm and the second way is to tap your underarm on the same side of your body.

PRACTICE

Try both ways of the underarm tapping point. Does one feel more comfortable than the other? Which way do you prefer?

Top of Head (TH) is located at the top of the head. Lightly tap the top of your head. Tapping on the top of the head can help release the inner critic and improve focus. This tapping point supports spiritual connection, insight, intuition, wisdom, as you bring forth clarity whilst regulating your nervous system.

PRACTICE

When we do a round of tapping, the sequence we generally will use is the side of hand, eyebrow, side of eye, under eye, under nose, chin, collarbone, underarm, and top of the head tapping points. Practice tapping on these points. Be curious as to how you like to tap. Do you like to use two hands? One hand? Alternate? Which feels comfortable for you?

Additional Tapping Points

Heart Centre (HC) is located at the centre of your chest, on your breastbone. Tapping on the heart centre can help relieve jealousy and the fear of being abandoned. This tapping point supports forgiveness, acceptance, compassion, and a sense of wholeness.

Wrist Point (WP) is located on either of the wrists. You can tap both wrist creases together, tap with two fingers or rub the creases together in a circular motion. Tapping on the wrist point can help release feelings of apprehension, grief, loss, and regret. This tapping point supports a deeper connection with oneself.

PRACTICE

I usually incorporate the heart centre and wrist points at the beginning or end of a tapping round. Practise tapping on these points. Do you like tapping on these points or rubbing them? Be curious as to how you like to tap with these points.

Gamut Point: The gamut point is found on the back of the hand. Find the area between your ring finger and middle finger. Then from the webbing between those fingers and move down about an inch. As you move toward the wrist, you should feel an indentation of where the point is.

Tapping on the Gamut point can help release trapped emotions within the body, calm the nervous system, and clear the mind. This tapping point supports positive thoughts and feelings, leading to a more holistic healing process.

There is a full method you can use with the Gamut Point, which is used with clients when tapping and the client's nervous system is overwhelmed in a high-extreme state. As this book is focused on the Foundations of Tapping, we won't focus on the 9 Gamut method. However, this point is mentioned as it is a great point to tap, rub on when stuck in an emotion, and do with some continual/ subtle tapping (chapter seven).

PRACTICE

Practise tapping on the gamut point. Do you like tapping on the gamut point, rubbing the gamut point, or a bit of both?

Finger Tapping Points

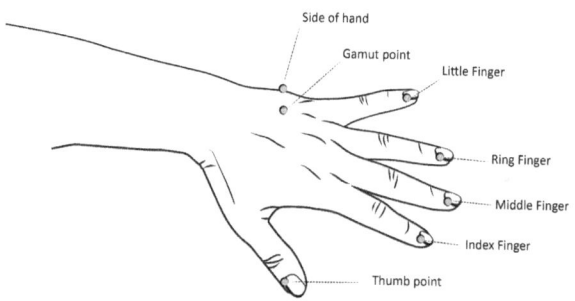

Thumb Point (TP) is located on the outside edge of your thumb just below the base of the thumbnail. Tapping on the thumb points can help release feelings of judgement towards yourself and others, as well as sadness. This tapping point supports humility and the balancing of emotions.

PRACTICE

To feel confident with finger tapping on the base of the nail. Tap your thumbs together.

FOUNDATIONS OF TAPPING

Index Finger (IF) is located on the base of your index fingernail closest to your body. Tapping on the index finger can help you let go of feelings of guilt, self-loathing, poor self-esteem, bitterness, anxiety, and pain. Tapping on this point supports self-love, empathy, intuition, and a positive outlook on life.

Middle finger (MF) is located on the base of your middle finger fingernail closest to your body. Tapping on the middle finger can release negative emotions such as sadness, grief, self-pity, and sorrow. Tapping on this point supports feelings of self-love, joy, satisfaction, as it soothes the heart, promoting compassionate communication, empathy, and excitement.

Ring Finger (RF) Tap on the side of the nail closest to you.

Little Finger (LF) (also known as the pinky finger) is located on the base of your little fingernail closest to your body. Tapping on the little finger helps release negative emotions such as depression, anger, jealousy, sadness, and anxiety. Tapping on this point supports emotional balance, tranquillity, gentleness, love, optimism, spiritual growth, and a revitalised zest for life.

PRACTICE

Tapping on the finger-tapping points is great to use at the end of a tapping round. Practice tapping on these points. Tapping on the finger points can be useful in situations when you are in public or perhaps even in a meeting etc. Do you like tapping on these points or rubbing them? Be curious as to how you like to tap with these points.

Reminders on tapping points

You can tap on all the tapping points using two fingers. If possible, tap a minimum of 5 to 7 times on a tapping point before moving to the next point. If you are unable to tap for any reason, you can also gently rub the tapping points in a circular motion, hold the points, and take a breath before moving on to the next point.

You can imagine you are tapping on the points. This is useful for people who want to tap without anyone knowing, or if you have pain in a particular tapping point.

Tapping hard does not make tapping more effective, so be gentle with yourself. You may feel a natural inclination to tap a certain way. It's possible you might sigh or take a deep breath when tapping too. Follow your intuition and tap on these points for as long as you feel drawn to do so. Pay attention to these points, as they might be the most beneficial for you in managing and supporting your emotions during difficult times.

PRACTICE

Allow yourself time to practise the tapping points and familiarise yourself with them. Become familiar with the points and see if you naturally just tap the main points, whether you naturally just do the finger points, all the points together, or something else.

Chapter Two

The Basic Recipe

PRACTICE

Give yourself permission to tap on the eyebrow point for one (1) minute whilst saying,

'*I am giving myself time and space to heal.*'

What is the Basic Recipe?

The Basic Recipe is the foundational tapping technique used in EFT. Tapping follows a sequence of steps called a round. Depending on the intensity of why you are tapping will dictate how many rounds of tapping you do. Dealing with persistent and profound emotional challenges is most effective when tapping is performed on a regular basis. The outcome will be optimised by tapping daily as the effects accumulate.

A round is where you tap on the side of hand, eyebrow, side of eye, under eye, under nose, chin, collarbone, underarm, and top of head points. Tapping a round can take roughly two minutes to complete. You can always add in the other tapping points in a round. The amazing thing about tapping is you can make it what you like.

In the Basic Recipe you:

1. Identify the Issue and the Emotion

2. Rate the Intensity – SUDS. (Subjective units of distress)

3. Create and tap on the set-up statement.

4. Tap your rounds using reminder phrases.

5. Rate the intensity again – SUDS.

6. Tap your rounds while repeating your affirmations and choices.

7. Rate the intensity again – SUDS.

8. Seal your tapping process with a deep inhale and exhale with a sigh.

9. Insights and Reflections.

How to do the Basic Recipe

1. Identify the Issue & the Emotion

The easiest way to start tapping is to bring awareness to an issue you'd like to focus on. The problem, issue, or challenge dominating your mental and emotional space in the present moment.

One or several things may come up. Know it is ok and there is no right or wrong. If you have several, I invite you to choose one. Use your intuition. It's ok. You can never make a wrong decision regarding this.

Some examples are:
- My workload is huge. I don't have enough time to do everything, and it is stressing me out.

- My body feels so sore and tired, and I feel drained.

- I got angry at my family and yelled at them. I can't stop thinking about it. I feel guilty and feel so awful.

FOUNDATIONS OF TAPPING

What issue, event, and/ or challenge is on your mind right now? Write them down on one of The Basic Recipe Worksheets from page 11 in the *Foundations of Tapping Companion Workbook*.

Once you have decided on the issue/ event/ challenge you would like to work on, become more specific. Without judgement, we want to bring in curiosity.

Now identify the emotion attached to that issue.

Here is a list of emotions[6] to support you in having a deeper understanding of your feelings and sensations. It is not an extensive list, so please know you don't have to choose only what is provided. The emotions list is also available on page 3 in the *Foundations of Tapping Companion Workbook*.

Uncertain	Sad	Sure
Confusion	Depressed	Strong
Upset	Desperate	Certain
Doubtful	Dejected	Unique
Uncertain	Heavy	Dynamic
Indecisive	Crushed	Tenacious
Perplexed	Disgusted	Hardy
Embarrassed	Upset	Secure
Hesitant	Hateful	Empowered
Shy	Sorrowful	Ambitious
Lost	Mournful	Powerful
Unsure	Weepy	Confident
Pessimistic	Frustrated	Bold
Tense		Determined

Happy	Anger	Energised
Amused	Annoyed	Determined
Delighted	Agitated	Inspired
Glad	Fed Up	Creative
Pleased	Irritated	Healthy
Charmed	Mad	Renewed
Grateful	Critical	Vibrant
Optimistic	Resentful	Strengthened
Content	Disgusted	Motivated
Joyful	Outraged	Focused
Enthusiastic	Raging	Invigorated
Loving	Furious	Refreshed
Marvellous	Livid	
	Bitter	

Once you have identified the emotion, notice where you feel it in your body and how your body may communicate this with you. You can do this by:

- Inviting yourself to close your eyes if you feel safe to do so. Otherwise, lower your gaze to a fixed point in front of you. Take a deep breath and check in with yourself by doing a slow body scan of your body from the top of your head to the tips of your toes.

- Notice where in your body the emotion is residing. Take note of any sensations, tensions, feelings of nothing at all, etc

- See, hear, feel and/or know if the emotion has

any colour, size, shape, texture, temperature, weight, smell, and/or taste.

Use your intuition. Remember this does not need to make logical sense to the mind, it is how the body feels.

It is also ok if your emotion does not have any colour, size, shape, texture, temperature, weight, smell, and/or taste. There is no right or wrong.

Use the Basic Recipe Worksheet in the *Foundations of Tapping Companion Workbook* from page 11 to write down the observations you make while tapping. Remember to use your own words and descriptions based on your experiences.

For example:

- 'I am sad after a breakup. This pain in my heart feels like someone has their hands tightened around my heart.'

- 'I feel uncertain about making a decision. I have a big coarse rope stuck in a knot in my stomach. The knot is the size of a two-story house'

- 'I feel lost in my throat. It is a big green, prickly ball the size of a basketball.'

- 'This anger I have feels like the back of my head is on fire. It smells like burnt hair'

- 'I feel overwhelmed with the amount of work I have to do. It is the colour purple and has the heaviness of 50kg weight plates on my shoulders.'

- 'I feel furious in my back. It is black in colour, the size of a car, shape of a triangle, prickly to touch, hot in temperature, and weighs a tonne'

Tapping success doesn't depend on having a comprehensive understanding of the emotions and physical sensations involved. Focusing on what you're feeling and tapping on it, even if you don't fully understand it, can lead to significant relief. If you're not sure what emotions you're feeling, take deep breaths and tap on the side of your hand, asking for the feeling to make itself known. If it is not clear, simply tap on 'this feeling' and see if it becomes clearer as you continue tapping.

The key is to tap, feel, and breathe.

2. Rate the Intensity – SUDS

We identify our Subject Units of Distress, our SUDS by:

1. On a scale from zero (0) to ten (10) with zero being no intensity and ten (10) being the most extreme. Rate the intensity of the emotion you're focusing on right now.

2. Now you know the issue and emotion you would like to tap on, I invite you to bring your attention to how it feels within your body and give it a number on a scale from 0 – 10. 10 being the most

intense and 0 being in no distress.

3. Don't think too deeply about what the number may be. There is no right or wrong answer. Use your intuition. The first number that comes to you when you bring awareness to your issue.

To support your healing journey when completing the *Foundations of Tapping Companion Workbook*, a summary identifying your SUDS is located on page 8.

3. Create and tap on the Set-up Statement

The Classic EFT Set-up Statement begins with, 'Even though,' followed by two parts. Part one is the issue you're focusing on; part two is a phrase of acceptance with the classic EFT statement being 'I completely and deeply love and accept myself.'

Example of part one: 'Even though I feel anxious about this presentation,' 'Even though I feel depressed,' or 'Even though I feel devastated someone crashed into my car and drove away without leaving any details.'

Example of part two: 'I completely and deeply love and accept myself.'

Begin by tapping, starting with the side of hand while saying the set-up statement. Then tap on all the tapping points in what is called a round.

When you have chosen a set-up statement, I invite you to take a deep breath in through the nose and out through the mouth with a sigh. Allow your breathing to return to normal. Begin tapping on the side of the hand. You can use either hand. Tap and repeat the full set-up statement three times.

Even though I (state your issue), I completely and deeply love and accept myself.

Even though I (state your issue), I completely and deeply love and accept myself.

Even though I (state your issue), I completely and deeply love and accept myself.

Some individuals who are suffering emotionally may struggle to express themselves because of feelings of intense shame or other obstacles. As such, they may have difficulty saying, 'I completely and deeply love and accept myself.' The amazing thing with EFT is that you can change these words to ones that may feel more comfortable. If you find this is the case, I suggest using the Choices Method created by Dr. Pat Carrington. [7]Bring forward the Choices Method where instead of 'I deeply and completely love and accept myself,' use 'I choose' instead.

Examples might be:

- 'Even though I feel extremely anxious right now, I like myself anyway.'

- 'Even though I feel afraid about heights, I honour my feelings.'

- 'Even though I feel pain in my shoulders, I allow myself to relax.'

- 'Even though I carry extra weight, I choose to consider the possibility that someday I may love and accept myself.'

FOUNDATIONS OF TAPPING

- 'Even though I am feeling sad and hopeless, I choose to allow myself to feel happy again.'
- 'Even though I am terrified to express myself with others, I choose to honour myself.'
- 'Even though I think I am a failure in life, I choose to release...'
- 'Even though I... I choose to let it go now.'
- 'Even though I... I choose to relax now.'
- 'Even though I... I allow my body to relax.'
- 'Even though I... I choose to release this feeling of (whatever you are feeling.)'
- 'Even though I... I choose to know I did the best I could under difficult circumstances.'

Forgiveness can have a profound healing effect, so you may want to consider incorporating it or using it as a substitute. An example is, 'Even though I feel rejected, I accept and forgive myself.'

Whichever way you choose for your set-up statement, repeat it three (3) times whilst tapping on your side of hand tapping point. It can be the same set-up statement for all three times, have the same first part of the set-up statement with three different second parts, or have three different set-up statements. Allow whatever wants to flow. The important thing to remember is there is no right or wrong.

4. Tap your rounds using reminder phrases

Begin a tapping round by tapping on the eyebrow point. As you tap your rounds you can say parts of the set-up statement either part one of the set-up statement and information you have already obtained regarding your emotions, where you feel them in your body (including sensations, tensions etc) what you see/ hear/ feel/ or know (including the colour, size, shape, texture, temperature, weight, smell, and taste) and your SUDS.

For example, if part of your set-up statement was 'I feel extremely anxious right now,' you might say when tapping on the eyebrow 'extremely anxious.' Then, as you tap on the side of eye tapping point, you may say 'anxiety,' and tapping under your eye, say 'feeling anxious in my chest.' Then tap under your nose and say 'It's an 8 out of 10', and so on.

With each round, tap on the eyebrow, side of eye, under eye, under nose, chin, collarbone, underarm, and top of head. You can also tap on the finger points during each round.

When finished with a round or two of tapping, allow yourself to take a deep inhale, exhale with a sigh, and take a sip of water. Maybe take note of any additional thoughts, feelings, sensations, reactions, or memories that come up. Notice particularly if they feel strong. Often, these are important clues as to what to tap on next. Tapping on these additional 'aspects' often unlocks the solution to your troubles. By addressing smaller, specific details of your memories, which are often at the root of your issue, you can gain clarity, experience greater peace and relaxation, and feel the confidence within as you continue living your life.

As you tap on your rounds, further information may arise about your event. Know you can tap on that information too. For example, after tapping, you may feel that underneath your feeling of being anxious is a realisation you are avoiding something.

5. Rate the Intensity Again – Check your SUDS

After you have done a round or two, you will then rate the intensity, and your SUDS again.

Take a moment to be in space with yourself, take in a deep breath, filling your belly with air, holding at the top before releasing with a sigh. Allow your body to move and/or stretch if it needs to.

Rate the intensity of the emotion you are focusing on and start tapping. Circle back to step 4 (You can start from step 3 if you prefer) and tapping for another round or two. Check-in to rate the intensity again. You continue this cycle until your SUDS get to a 2 or lower. It is normal not to feel any significant change after only one round of tapping.

If your rating is going down, that is a great sign. Keep tapping, circling back to step 4, and tapping for another round. You ideally want to get to 3 or lower where you then bring your affirmations and emotions to ground.

If your rating is rising, that is a good sign too.

Sometimes when energy is stuck and has been impacted deep within us, it needs to rise before it can flow through and release. If this occurs, please keep tapping, circling back to step 4 (you can start from step 3 if you prefer), and tapping for another round.

If your rating is staying the same, know there is nothing wrong with that. This is an opportunity to be more curious about the questions surrounding how you're feeling and keep tapping, circling back to step 4 (you can start from step 3 if you prefer), and tapping for another round.

You've checked in on your SUDS, and your intensity rating, now check in on how you feel. How do you feel about it now?

It's normal to experience emotions after a challenging event or when reminiscing about a difficult period in your life. Take note of the emotions you're feeling (such as anxiety, grief, anger, frustration, etc), as you can use them in your next round of tapping. Using your own words and tapping on your emotions can make a significant difference. Although it may be easier to identify your thoughts, it's crucial to acknowledge your feelings. If necessary, refer to the list of emotions to help you identify what you are feeling.

It is important to keep in mind that blocked energies often have multiple layers. The deeper emotions or thoughts may be hidden beneath the surface. The beliefs and feelings you experience on the surface are often just symptoms of deeper-seated issues. As you use tapping, pay close attention to the flow of your energy.

FOUNDATIONS OF TAPPING

Here are some questions that can support you as you uncover and address the underlying core issues.
- Do you feel more clarity?
- What is the fear beneath this? What is deeper than that? Is there a deeper layer?

If you feel the statement changing, finish tapping through the original statement, then tap for the new, clearer level of the issue.

Tapping helps to unblock and facilitate smoother energy flow in your energy field. It's a powerful and successful method for releasing trapped energy caused by thoughts and beliefs that don't align with you. As you utilise this technique more frequently, you'll notice a change in your awareness and consciousness. Your patterns and the roots of your emotional and mental tendencies will become clearer, and you'll have a greater understanding of your core issues, allowing you greater ease in releasing them in the present moment.

6. Tap your rounds on Affirmations and Choices

As you tap through your rounds, however many that may be, you might be feeling a lot calmer and more relaxed. What I love to do once I've done a few rounds of tapping, even perhaps when my number is a 3 or below, is to begin to move into choices and affirmations.

For affirmations and choices, it is important to stop and reflect after your tapping rounds:
- How do I want to feel about this situation?

- What would I like to happen?
- How would I like to respond?

Maybe it is the desire to want to feel calm, relaxed, or happy, or to know you did the best you could in a difficult situation?

Acknowledge the initial feeling and how you wish it would feel as you move into the next round of tapping.

Examples of affirmations and choices are:
- I am good enough.
- I am valuable.
- It is safe for me to relax.
- I am worthy.
- I am worthy of love.
- I trust myself.
- I am heard.
- I can meet my needs.
- I am safe in the world.
- I have enough.
- I love myself.

- It is safe to speak my truth.
- I am open to receive.
- I am supported.
- I am confident.
- I am loved.
- I am not too old/ too young.
- My body size does not define me.
- I am enough.
- My presence is enough.
- I am confident.
- I am strong.
- I am powerful.
- All I need is within me right now.
- I am getting better and better every day.
- I am living in abundance.
- I am filled with focus.
- I am smart/ pretty/ talented.
- I am constantly growing and evolving.

- I am freeing myself from all destructive doubt and fear.
- I am healing and strengthening every day.
- I choose not to compare myself to others.
- I choose to be happy.
- I forgive myself.
- I accept myself for who I am and create peace, power, and confidence of mind and heart.
- I feel more grateful each day.
- I can make a difference.
- I am proud of myself.
- I believe in myself.
- I am fearless.
- I can do this.
- I have the power to change my story.
- I have the courage to say 'No.'
- I am fearless.
- I am in awe of what my body is capable of.
- I am open to receiving.

FOUNDATIONS OF TAPPING

- I trust my intuition.
- I trust my journey.
- I am supported.

PRACTICE

Go to page 4 in the **Foundations of Tapping Companion Workbook** *and list some affirmations and choices you want to include in your tapping to support your grounding and feeling of safety.*

Now tap on the choices and affirmations you have chosen.

In these last few rounds, tap on what you would rather choose in your life, as this can be powerful.

- I choose to be happy.
- I am filled with focus.
- I am proud of myself.
- I trust myself.
- I am confident.

For example, when it comes to being nervous about

giving a presentation, the affirmations and choices rounds may include:
EB: I am confident.
SOE: I am feeling calm.
UE: I'm looking forward to this presentation.
UN: I believe in what I am saying.
CH: I know the content and I can do this.
CB: I can do this presentation.
UA: I believe in myself.
TOH: I'm feeling calm.

With each choice and affirmation tapping, use the ones that connect and resonate with what you are tapping about. Allow it to also become specific for you.

You can use the same words or phrases for example saying, 'I can do this' for a whole round. There is no right or wrong.

By incorporating affirmations and choices into tapping, we can effectively implant our desired personal preferences into our subconscious mind, which heavily influences our daily actions and reactions through established patterns and habits.

7. Rate the intensity again – check SUDS

After you have done a round or two, again what feels comfortable for you, you will then rate the intensity, and your SUDS again.

Always take a moment to be in space with yourself, take in a deep breath, fill your belly with air, hold at the top, and exhale with a sigh. Keep alternating between rounds 7 and 8 until you are at least a 2 or below in your SUDS.

Once you have a rating of 1 or 2, ask yourself if you still wish to hold on to the 1 or 2 SUDS or to release it. Allow yourself to use your intuition. If you feel like releasing it, repeat steps 7 and 8 as many times as needed until your SUD becomes a 0.

If you are happy to allow the 1 or 2 to remain, please know this is ok. There is no right or wrong.

8. Seal your tapping process with a deep inhale and exhale with a sigh

Once you have your 0 SUDS or your 1 or 2 SUD rating that you are happy to keep, allow yourself to deeply through the nose. As your belly fills with air, hold your breath at the top and exhale with a sigh. Allow your body to move if it wishes to move.

9. Insights and reflections

When we tap and attune to ourselves, our bodies, and our emotions, we can at times reveal a limiting belief, a deeper understanding, a deeper knowing, another layer to what we are tapping about. Awareness may bring forth understanding and forgiveness for yourself. Please know after tapping there is always the invitation to continue writing in your journal with any insights and/or reflections. It doesn't have to be much or in-depth if you are not a writer. It's a great way to see growth within yourself.

Also know, the insights and reflections don't have to

come to you right away. It can be some time afterward and know that is ok. With newfound awareness and understanding from tapping into your emotions, you have the power to replace any limiting belief with the empowering knowledge you are worthy of experiencing love and allowing it into your life.

To support your healing journey when completing the *Foundations of Tapping Companion Workbook*, a summary of the SUDS is located on page 8 and the summary of the Basic Recipe is located on page 9.

PRACTICE

*Try the Basic Recipe using the worksheets provided in the **Foundations of Tapping Workbook** from page 11. Allow the release of what is ready to let go from your body. Ideally, choose an issue/ event/ experience/ challenge you feel able to do by yourself, to begin with, and know you can make this however you want it to be. There is no right or wrong.*

Information on Tapping

Why do we pay attention to our emotions while we are tapping?

We bring awareness to the emotions surrounding the issue/ event/ challenge we are tapping on as well as the emotion we feel within us at that time. It can be challenging to recognise and understand one's emotions, as our thoughts often dominate our awareness. However, it's crucial to acknowledge intense emotions trigger our instinctual survival response, putting us in a state of fight, flight, freeze, or fawn (trauma responses). These, which can hinder our ability to make rational and well-thought-out decisions. By reducing the intensity of these emotions through tapping, it becomes easier to think clearly and take proactive steps toward what we desire in life. The more precise we can be about identifying our emotions, the more beneficial our tapping experience can be.

Why tap on the negative?

People may have concerns about tapping on the negative thinking it is going to manifest more negativity in their life. However, it is quite the opposite.

In the basic recipe, we tap on the negative before tapping on the choices, the affirmations, and the grounding. It is crucial to address negative thoughts and beliefs at the subconscious level as they often contain limiting reasons for why we don't deserve what we want, why it feels impossible to attain, or why it is unsafe to pursue our desires, leading to the attraction of more of what we don't want. Tapping helps to relax the energetic hold these limiting beliefs, painful emotions, and traumatic memories have on us, enabling us to align with what we truly desire. By releasing these unconscious self-sabotaging patterns, tapping enables us to tap into our aspirations and affirmations, and attract positivity into our lives. Until we address the negative emotional charge caused by challenging circumstances, the manifestation of our desired outcomes will remain difficult.

Change is possible!

What happens if other Issues/ Events/ Challenges come up in a tapping round?

Perhaps while tapping, another memory of when you were angry came up. Or you recalled the time you were hurt or felt scared, and it had nothing to do with the issue you were tapping on. If so, make note of it so you can remember to tap on it another time.

Why is tapping not working?

Sometimes people may tap and say this isn't working, why? If this is happening, please know you are not doing anything wrong. Sometimes for energy to shift, we look at what we have been tapping on and ask, 'Have I been specific enough?'

Maybe slow down a little. Close your eyes and tune

in to how your body is feeling. Tapping shifts energy in our subtle body and it's not until we attune to our body that we may notice the subtle changes. Are you inhaling more deeply? Feeling lighter on the shoulders? Is the tension in your jaw easing? Or perhaps even changing aspects? Sometimes feelings and emotions change i.e., feeling dissociated from life to being able to feel something.

Ask yourself, is there any resistance? For someone who may have been in survival mode or autopilot for so long, there may be a subconscious resistance. For example, a sense of calm or safety can feel different, completely out of your comfort zone. Underneath the resistance is there a limiting belief, a fear within the subconscious, towards change or the unknown? Perhaps a limiting belief you are not worthy to feel this way is an example.

Sometimes we may need to ask different questions while tapping to see what may arise. Some examples you can use are:

- What was going on when this began?

- What does this issue/ event/ challenge remind me of?

- If I could place an emotion on this issue/ emotion/ challenge, what would it be?

- What have I been told about this issue/ event/ challenge?

- What do I believe about this issue/ event/ challenge?

- Does this remind me of another time in the past when I felt this way?

- Check-in to see if any beliefs are keeping this emotion from discharging, i.e., it's not ok to let go of this anger because what he/she did was wrong, etc.

Sometimes we may subconsciously resist/ block/ deflect wanting to go deeper within our tapping. If this happens know it is ok. You haven't done anything wrong and there is nothing wrong with you. Your nervous system may require more grounding, resourcing, and a felt sense of safety before it can continue to go deeper. An appropriate Practitioner can guide and support you through this process.

An Example of the Basic Recipe

Below is an actual example of the basic recipe I did when I was annoyed at being late for an appointment.

Step 1: Identifying the issue and emotion.
I want to tap on how annoyed I am for being late for an appointment this morning.
I feel annoyed and underneath this emotion is anger.
I feel angry.
I feel this anger in my face.
Right side of my face, dark black cloud, looks like a rock and the size of my hand. It feels rough and it has no smell or taste.
I want to grind my teeth.

Step 2: Rate the intensity - SUDS.
8/10

Step 3: Create and tap on set up statement.
SOH: Even though I feel angry right now for being late for an appointment this morning, I deeply and completely love and accept myself.
SOH: Even though I am so angry right now to the right side of my face where I have this black cloud, all from being late for an appointment, I deeply and completely love and honour myself.
SOH: Even though I am filled with so much anger

because I was late for an appointment this morning, and now have this rock size cloud at the side of my face, I deeply and completely love and accept myself, just as I am.

Step 4: Tap your rounds while saying out loud.
EB: Angry.
SOE: I feel so angry right now.
UE: For being late for an appointment.
UN: And it's an 8/10.
CH: I'm so angry.
CB: And it's making me want to grind my teeth.
UA: As the anger takes the right side of my face.
TOH: Anger in this black cloud.

EB: Anger in this rock, the size of my fist.
SOE: It's rough to touch.
UE: I am so angry.
UN: All from being late for an appointment.
CH: Why am I late?
CB: I was rushing.
UA: I wasn't ready in time.
TOH: And now I am angry.

Step 5: Take a deep breath and check in on SUDS.
Now a 6/10.
Any changes?
The cloud is raining.
And a dark grey.
Blame.

Blame myself.

Step 4: Tap doing more rounds.
EB: I feel blame.
SOE: Blame towards myself.
UE: For being late for this appointment.
UN: A 6/10.
CH: My black cloud is now a dark grey cloud that is raining.
CB: I can't even get to an appointment on time.
UA: I got all the kids ready.
TOH: Even rushed through getting myself ready.

EB: And was still late.
SOE: I can't even get to a place on time.
UE: I can't even get to a place on time for me.
UN: And I was late.
CH: And nearly missed my appointment.
CB: I can't do anything right.
TOH: I'm such a failure.

Step 5: Take a deep breath and check in on SUDS.
I blame myself because I nearly missed the appointment. Rushing and was still late.

A slight perception that has come in was, does it matter if I was late? Why am I holding onto this anger? It is already done.

Light grey cloud, still raining, rock has gone smaller, still rough, 4/10.

Step 4: Tapping rounds.
EB: This anger and blame.
SOE: Still on the side of my face.
UE: Light grey cloud is still raining.
UN: But the rock has is now smaller.
CH: And it is a 4/10.
CB: I blame myself for being late. It's all my fault.
UA: I nearly missed my appointment.
TOH: Does it matter that I was late? The appointment still happened. Why am I holding onto this?

EB: Where I am feeling like I am such a failure?
SOE: Am I really a failure just for being late?
UE: No, but I am disappointed.
UN: I don't like being late, I like being early.
CH: And I worry what others thought about me being late?
CB: And I held the anger and blame towards me all day.
UA: I still hold it now.
TOH: So, I didn't enjoy the day.

Step 5: Take a deep breath and check in on SUDS.
3/10.
Any changes?
Sun shower off white cloud, small rock, still rough to touch.
I was angry at myself all day for a mistake I made.

Step 6: Tap using affirmations and choices.

EB: I made a mistake.
SOE: I am not perfect.
UE: And I don't have to be perfect.
UN: It's ok to make mistakes.
CH: That's what makes me human.
CB: I must remind myself this.
TOH: It's ok to make mistakes.

EB: I don't need to be so harsh on myself.
SOE: So angry on myself for making a mistake.
UE: I forgive myself.
UN: I forgive myself for being late.
CH: I am worthy of love.
UA: Worthy to give myself love.
TOH: Even when I make mistakes.
HC: I am worthy of love.
HC: Even when I make mistakes.

Step 7: Take a big breath and check in on SUDS.
1/10.
Any changes?
White cloud on the side of my face, the cloud feels soft.
After the rain, the sun shines, and my faces is filled with light. My jaw isn't tight, and I don't want to clench my teeth. In fact, I want to smile.

Step 8: Seal your tapping process with a deep inhale and exhale with a sigh.

Step 9: Any insights or reflections.
As I was tapping I saw how my perfectionism likes to sneak in. I need to be kinder to myself. I was late. Mistakes happen and being so angry at myself wasn't going to change the situation.

It would be good to add tapping on my perfectionism another time. To dive deeper through the layers. Even working through some events in my Personal Peace Procedure. (Which is described later in chapter four.)

Chapter Three

Tapping through the Layers

PRACTICE

Give yourself permission to tap on the side of eye point for one (1) minute whilst saying,

'I am whole in every phase I am in.'

Limiting Beliefs

When we go through the layers and reach the root structure, we can meet with a limiting belief. Limiting beliefs are thoughts and opinions we believe to be the absolute truth. [8]They are subconscious thoughts creeping in and telling us something is ultimately true. By believing our limiting beliefs, we are ultimately placing limitations on our abilities.

Some examples of limiting beliefs are:
- I am alone.
- I am a burden.
- I am not good enough.
- I am a failure.
- Nobody loves me/ I am unlovable/ I will never be loved.
- I am not smart/ pretty/ talented enough.
- I am too old/ too young.
- I don't deserve success/ I don't deserve ....
- I am not worthy.
- I am stupid.

- I am not skinny enough.
- I have to be perfect.
- No one will like me because ....
- I am not enough on my own.
- My opinion is not important.
- No one listens to me.
- I will never find ....
- I never get opportunities to ....
- I fear conflict.
- Life is hard.
- I can't deal with this.
- What will they think of me?
- It won't work anyway.
- Why bother even trying?
- I give up.
- Life is unfair.

Limiting beliefs are assumptions about your reality within your subconscious and come from your perceptions of life experiences. An experience in the present day can trigger an unresolved emotional response.

These beliefs can be triggered according to specific events that may have made you suffer in the past as well as trauma you are not consciously aware including generational trauma. When experiencing a limiting belief your behaviour may change to include procrastination, conformism, overthinking, anxiety, imposter syndrome, and other reactions because of your subconscious trying to avoid/ cope with the trigger.

For example, if you were called to the boss's office for a talk, it can transport you back to a time in primary school when you had to attend the principal's office for a talk because you were in trouble, or thought you were in trouble. Or you saw someone else having to go to the principal's office for a talk as they got into big trouble, regardless of whether you are consciously aware of the connection. This can bring the thoughts and feelings from the experience of the principal's office flooding back into your body and mind, leading to similar physical responses, emotional reactions, and limiting beliefs.

As you tap on any issues/ events/ challenges, you may become aware of a limiting belief, and see a pattern of the same limiting belief come up. If you do, please don't be afraid. This is your body letting you know you are ready to go deeper and release the layers. You are ready to up level, and your consciousness is ready to expand.

Fears that common limiting beliefs come back to:
- Fear of responsibility/ commitment.
- Fear of change.
- Fear of abandonment.
- Fear of disapproval.
- Fear of rejection.
- Fear of vulnerability.
- Fear of not being good enough.
- Fear of power.
- Fear of unworthiness.
- Fear of humiliation.
- Fear of own humanity.
- Fear of death.

PRACTICE

*Are you aware of your limiting beliefs? Do you resonate with any of the limiting beliefs just by reading them? Go to page 26 within your **Foundations of Tapping Companion Workbook** and write down any limiting beliefs you are currently aware of. You may find a pattern appearing here. If any arise as you continue through the book, come back, and write them down.*

If you become aware of a limiting belief, you can ask the following questions, developed in the Work of Byron Katie[9], allowing an answer to present. Tap on the answers and see/ hear/ feel/ or know the response. You can ask these questions and answer them whilst tapping:

1. Is this true?

2. Can you absolutely know that to be true?

3. How do you react? What happens when you believe this thought?

4. Who would you be without that thought?

Sometimes the answers reveal themselves straight away, and at other times, they come up during integration and you'll have an aha moment. Again, there

FOUNDATIONS OF TAPPING

is no right or wrong way.

There may be limiting beliefs you wish to hold on to, and you may have some resistance letting go. This is quite normal, and it's where tapping can help you transform by removing secondary gain around these beliefs.

Secondary Gain

A secondary gain is a benefit that comes from a certain issue/ event/ or challenge. It is the subconscious motivators we may have from not overcoming or releasing the issue. It can be the reason we may appear stuck and not making the expected progress within our healing journey. When secondary gain is present, it is harder for us to change because we are losing the benefit from the issue.[10]

The subconscious resistance to holding onto an issue/ event/ or challenge is also its way of trying to protect you from losing some type of control your nervous system feels it had.

Some examples of a secondary gain are:
- A person suffering with chronic pain may not find pleasure in socialising with their partner's friends. When the pain becomes unbearable, their partner refrains from urging them to attend social gatherings.

- A person gets more encouragement and caring

comments from their friends the longer they stay distressed.

- A person may receive financial support from the government due to their illness and may heavily rely on it as their primary source of income. In the event of their recovery, the financial benefit they depend on may cease.

- A person may experience a significant amount of anxiety and fear about both succeeding and failing. They recognise making changes could open up opportunities for greater success, but the idea of stepping out of their comfort zone leaves them feeling uneasy.

What to do if you have a secondary gain?
If you become aware you have a secondary gain, firstly be gentle with yourself. Having a secondary gain is not a negative reflection on your personality. We all have secondary gains in life.

If you feel you have a secondary gain to an issue/ event/ challenge, allow yourself to be in a comfortable place where you feel safe. Spend a few minutes breathing slowly. Inhale through the nose for four seconds and exhale through either the nose or mouth, whichever feels comfortable for you, and allow the exhale for six seconds. Tap on the side of your hand or tap on your gamut point and ask yourself, 'What could be the reason for wanting this issue?'

Allow space to see/ hear/ feel or know what may come through for you.

If you want more support, you can ask yourself the following questions developed by Stewart Robertson[11]:

- What are the possible upsides to holding this issue?

- What are the downsides to having a solution?

- What happened the last time you achieved this solution?

- Will others know who you are without this issue? Will you know who you are without this issue?

- In what way will having this issue make you seem unimportant? Too similar? Too different? Or something else?

- In what way will not having this issue be unsafe? Dangerous? Stressful? Insecure? Uncertain? Unfamiliar? Or something else?

- Will having the solution change your expectations of you?

- Will it change your expectations of yourself?

Going through these questions regarding a secondary gain will allow you to find the deeper issue. A subconscious fear, a trauma, and/ or limiting belief you can then tap on.

Know that tapping can support you in releasing your secondary gains so you can continue your healing journey.

Gratitude

We can feel, be and act grateful. However, while you are on your healing journey, tapping through fear and trauma, gratitude can at times feel less natural. Cultivating a practice of gratitude allows us to experience joy and gratefulness even at times when life may not be going according to plan.

PRACTICE

What are 3 things that make you feel grateful?

Tapping Tree

You may find as you tap through your rounds, different layers or aspects will reveal themselves. If you need support as you go through the layers, I would love for you to use the Tapping Tree.

FOUNDATIONS OF TAPPING

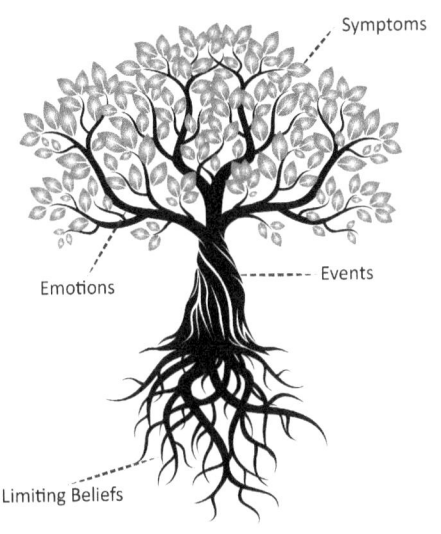

The Tapping Tree is made up of four parts – the leaves, branches, trunk, and roots. Each of these can correspond to what we can tap upon. The Tapping Tree was designed by Lindsay Kenny and introduced by Nick Ortner in his Tapping Solution[12] Book.

The Tapping Tree is a great way to support you as you tap through the layers. It may bring awareness to what you are feeling in a visual way.

Name your Tapping Tree: To begin your Tapping Tree, give what you are feeling a title. As we saw in the Basic Recipe, it is best to be specific.

For example: Instead of saying, I feel sad, be a little more specific. Example: I feel sad when I try on my best dress because it is now too tight.

Once you have your title, go through the tree, and see

what comes up for you.

Leaves: Physical Symptoms or other side effects of the issue.

The leaves represent the symptoms we feel from our issue or problem. It may be physical pain or symptoms of anxiety such as tension in shoulders, busy thoughts, upset stomach. By tapping on these symptoms, we can alleviate or eliminate them.

Branches: Feelings and the emotions you are experiencing.

The branches represent our emotions or feelings. Every issue or problem will bring with it an emotion whether it is sadness, grief, anger, stress, frustration, or fear. When we tap on our emotions, we reduce the intensity. As a result, it allows our capacity within our nervous system to expand and become regulated.

The Trunk: Events we use as proof and historical fact.

The trunk is a representation of an actual event or situation. It may be a situation that has yet to happen or a current event. Tapping on what has happened or what may happen in the future will help clear the impact it may be having on us.

The Roots: Limiting Beliefs; all those stories we think are true.

The roots hold the tree together and they represent our underlying beliefs about ourselves.

We can tap on any of these parts. Remember, the tree can survive and continue to grow even if its leaves are removed, branches are cut, or if it is felled at the trunk.

However, it is only when we take the roots away that the tree will no longer exist.

An Example of a Tapping Tree

Below is an example of mine using the Tapping Tree.

Name your Tapping Tree
I feel sad when I try on my best dress because it is now too tight.
Leaves: Physical Symptoms or other side effects of the issue.
My heart is beating fast. I have been eating more snacks since I stopped drinking alcohol. Thoughts that I am obese.
Branches: Feelings and the emotions you feel about the issue.
Feeling sadness, disgust towards my stomach and thighs, guilt, rejection, and depression.
The Trunk: Events we use as proof and historical fact.
My body shape has changed because I cannot fit into my dress.
The Roots: Limiting Beliefs; all those stories we think are true.
My self-worth is based on my weight. I am ugly. I am not lovable.
What happens after you do your tapping tree?
When you have completed your tapping tree, use the

Basic Recipe to tap through the layers. You may start at the leaves, followed by the branches, trunk, and roots. You may go straight to the root of the tree or something else. Do what you feel your nervous system has the capacity for. If something is outside of the scope to do yourself, you can always do this with an appropriate EFT Practitioner.

Know it is ok if you don't answer everything on your Tapping Tree whilst filling it out. More things may come to you as you tap on the parts of your Tapping Tree you have filled out.

PRACTICE

*Go to page 29 in the **Foundations of Tapping Companion Workbook** where you will find the Tapping Tree worksheet. Use the Tapping Tree worksheet with the Basic Recipe worksheet to support you in working with your Tapping Tree.*

Chapter Four

Personal Peace Procedure

PRACTICE

Give yourself permission to tap on the under eye point for one (1) minute whilst saying,

'*I am worthy of love and abundance.*'

What is the Personal Peace Procedure?

Gary Craig also created the Personal Peace Procedure, a method of addressing and releasing the emotional impact of past events. This process involves creating a list of negative experiences such as regrets, traumas, and current issues, and then using tapping to relieve their energy. This can lead to an increase in feelings of relaxation, positivity, and peace allowing you to become more. More empowered, calmer, feeling as though you are responding to things better as you have worked towards building a flexible autonomous nervous system.

The Personal Peace Procedure helps us organise and work through our past, allowing us freedom from our limiting emotions.

There may be fear or reluctance around approaching these events. Usually, these fears can be handled as you work through the procedure. If at any time you feel this may overwhelm your nervous system, please book in for a 1:1 session with an appropriate Practitioner.

How to do the Personal Peace Procedure

Begin your Personal Peace Procedure by grabbing your *Foundations of Tapping Companion Workbook* from page 58 and list all the experiences in your life you wished you could have skipped. Give them all a short title, a movie title, just enough to remind you of the issue.

For example:
- Getting fired.
- Getting grounded by Mum.
- Falling over at the bus stop.
- Failing the maths exam.
- That babysitter.
- Being bullied in Year 6.
- Falling over at the school race.

We don't want you to delve into the specifics here. It's a broad, 'movie title' style list. Not an emotional dive into your past.

Regardless of the size or perceived significance of an experience, if it elicits emotions such as sadness, fear, frustration, shame, or rejection, it is worth writing it down and addressing it through tapping. Keeping track of your progress in this way will allow you to see how you respond instead of reacting, as what may have once held strong emotional intensity loses its power.

Next to the title you have given this, also place the intensity rating, your SUDS out of 10. Remember 10 is the most intense and 0 being nothing.

What I personally like to add is a traffic light system developed by Seth Porges,[13] which is commonly used with trauma and the nervous system. I suggest the traffic light system because my service as an Intuitive Trauma Release Mentor is to not re-traumatise you and this method will allow some safety.

Red are experiences which are an extreme overwhelm to your nervous system. You don't even want to go near them. For these experiences, please book in a 1:1 session with an appropriate Practitioner. There are many other tapping techniques that can be used for traumatic, overwhelming, complicated and beyond experiences best done with the knowledge of an appropriate Practitioner.

Yellow are experiences you feel are overwhelming, complicated, or connected to other events and you may prefer to have support. I recommend tapping with a an appropriate Practitioner.

Green are the experiences you feel comfortable doing yourself. 'I can work on this.'

Even if some experiences or memories may seem trivial at first, it is still valuable to record them. The mere fact they came to mind indicates a potential for resolution and improvement through tapping.

Be gentle and take your time as you work towards placing 100 on your list. It sounds like a lot, however, over time your list will grow. As you start to write, you may see how effortless it is.

You can organise the experiences, your movie titles, in whatever way you like. You might group them with subheadings such as primary school, high school, university, job, etc. You may have subheadings under specific people such as mum, dad, brother, sister, teacher, coach. Do whatever feels comfortable for you.

If an experience, no matter how small you believe it is, comes to mind, write it down.

PRACTICE

Write down as many movie titles as you can using the worksheets provided in the **Foundations of Tapping Companion Workbook** *from page 58 followed by the SUDs and traffic light rating. Try not to be fixated on the number. Remember, there is no right or wrong.*

What happens after you create your list?

Now you have your list, *choose one to work on.* Preferably from the green traffic light system.

You can then go through the basic recipe in EFT

Tapping.

Sometimes, within our list we may find an issue with a limiting belief attached to it whether we are consciously or subconsciously aware.

Remember, if a limiting belief comes up, you can ask the questions developed in the work of Byron Katie. You can also go back to the Limiting Beliefs here and in the *Foundations of Tapping Companion Workbook* (Chapter Three).

Pay attention to other specific details of your chosen event/moment that may arise during your tapping. Make a note of them but continue with your selected event. Don't be tempted to chase the new thought that has popped into your head. Stick with the event you are working on.

Make a note of any positive shifts in your experience. Without awareness of your progress, the positive changes that come from tapping may go unnoticed. However, when you start to see the benefits of this process, you will probably be motivated to continue and make time for it in the future.

If, for any reason, you do not feel safe or you are not comfortable exploring these events on your own, please seek the support of an appropriate Practitioner.

Benefits of doing the Personal Peace Procedure

The more you tap, the quicker you will experience relief. This enables you to focus on creating the life you desire and making positive, conscious choices. You don't have to work through every issue or memory, as focusing on a few can often resolve many others in the generalisation effect.

Don't be discouraged by a long list of challenging experiences in your past. You don't have to tackle everything to experience significant peace and relief. With tapping, there's no need to be triggered, re-traumatised, or repeatedly recount painful memories. Once you've worked through the aspects of a particular memory, you can continue living your life, leaving what is not serving you behind.

What is the Generalisation Effect?

When you make progress with EFT, you may find a phenomenon Tapping known as the Generalisation Effect[14], where reducing the emotional charge of one memory can ease the emotional impact of similar memories. It's common to find some items on your list no longer affect you, even without direct tapping.

Picture bowling pins at the end of an alley. As you

bowl the ball, it hits one pin, which ultimately hits and knocks down other pins. By tapping on one event to release its emotional charge, you may release the emotional charge of other events.

Reminders for the Personal Peace Procedure

Approach these events in your own time and in your own way whilst being gentle with yourself.

Stick with the one event/moment you started with until your intensity level is less than 3.

Sometimes you may have to tap on a particular memory a few times to address all aspects of the memory. For instance, if you experienced bullying, you may have feelings towards the bully, and towards friends who didn't defend you, a family member who laughed at you, and even a teacher who didn't support you. By tapping on all aspects of the incident and any emotions attached to it, allows for full emotional release. After addressing your earliest memory of being bullied, you may find the Generalisation Effect has taken place and subsequent related experiences no longer hold an emotional charge, even though you didn't tap on them directly.

If you are finding a memory or moment too intense or painful to deal with on your own and you don't want to avoid it, now may be the time for you to get assistance from a qualified Practitioner.

Always remember when tapping to pay attention to your body. Do you feel lighter and/ or clearer? Are you beginning to feel surprisingly relieved in ways you never thought possible? Are you breathing more easily? Feeling less stressed? More energised? Less tension in your body? Ask yourself, 'What is different?'

Consider what you might do differently now in relation to this event and its effects. For example, if you tapped on being in a car accident, notice what might be different for you in relation to that car accident now.

You will find as you tap your way through your Personal Peace Procedure list that by clearing many of the larger issues, the smaller issues no longer seem to have any charge. Think of a house of cards, where each card holds a memory. As we tap on the bottom cards, they loosen and collapse, taking with them the events and memories that caused you pain, sometimes for many years. Imagine clearing one issue a day for the whole year! That's 365 troubling bothersome memories released.

PRACTICE

*Go to page 61 in the **Foundations of Tapping Companion Workbook** and use the Basic Recipe worksheets to support you with a movie title using the traffic light system.*

Chapter Five

Chakra Tapping

PRACTICE

Give yourself permission to tap on the under nose point for one (1) minute whilst saying,

'In each phase of my life, I am worthy and whole.'

What is a Chakra?

Chakra is a Sanskrit word that translates to 'circle' or 'wheel.' In our western system, the chakras correspond with the colours of the rainbow, with red at the base and violet at the crown.

The 7 chakra centres in our body are energetic vortexes that are in constant motion (wheel). They serve as storage for old stories, experiences, and memories, making them a useful entry point for identifying any limiting beliefs that may be holding us back. When our body becomes stuck in stress/ fear/ trauma, it creates an imbalance in one or more of our chakras.

Our chakras vibrate at a particular frequency, each individual energy wheel having a specific mind-body-spirit association. Tapping with your chakras allows you to tune into your own vibrational emotional, mental, physical, and spiritual bodies to release stuck energy. When the chakras are spinning in a natural healthy state you will experience peace, authenticity, congruency and truly enjoy your life.

Location of the Chakras

To understand chakra's, it is best to know where they are located within your body along with their corresponding tapping point.

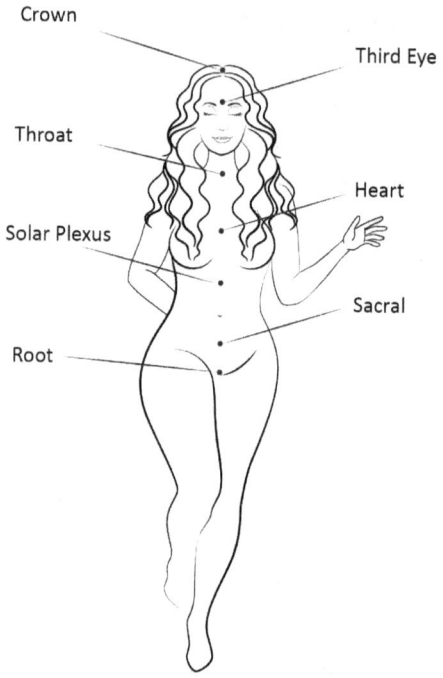

Root Chakra: The root chakra is located at the base of the spine between the anus and genitals and its core is basic trust. It is grounding energy and represents the time of creation, purpose, humility, and community. When our root chakra is out of balance, we can feel unsafe and not trusting, insecure, humiliated, feel like our life is in chaos, and living in survival mode.

Sacral Chakra: The sacral chakra is located within the pelvis behind the navel in the lower abdomen area and its core is sexuality and creativity. Here lies feminine energy, the catalyst for the movement of creation, the flowing of life, including your personal choices and actions. When our sacral chakra is out of balance, we can be in denial, feel disappointed in ourselves, can experience different addictions, unhealthy habits, and people-pleasing.

Solar Plexus Chakra: The solar plexus chakra is located just below the sternum and its core is wisdom and power. It governs your sense of personal power, your confidence, self-esteem, and surrender. When we feel out of balance with our solar plexus chakra, we can feel little or no self-worth, have resistance to receiving support, and/ or resistance to our own expansion and evolution. Hiding our vulnerability to protect ourselves from the fear of rejection, hiding our shame, and at times, lowering our boundaries in hopes love will be reciprocated.

Heart Chakra: The heart chakra is located at the centre of your chest and its core is love and healing as it comes from a place of nurturing and care. It is all about love, intimacy, forgiveness, acceptance, wholeness, and compassion, with the ability to send and receive love. Its focus is love, relationships, and inner healing. When we feel out of balance within our heart chakra, we can feel unforgiving, bitter, jealous, and believe we have been abandoned.

Throat Chakra: The throat chakra is located at the base of your throat. This chakra is about communication. It is all about open and honest expression, communication, and truth, and it allows creative manifestation. Believing in your faith and choosing from love. When we feel out of balance within our throat chakra, we can feel like we have lost faith in life, dissociated, and living in the choices we make out of fear.

Third Eye Chakra: The third eye chakra is located directly between the eyebrows and its core is awareness. It represents intuition, imagination, reflection, and the receiving of your inner guidance. When we feel out of balance with our third eye chakra, we can feel separated from life itself. We can feel lost as we become spiritually weakened and see life in tunnel vision.

Crown Chakra: The crown chakra is located on the top of the head and its core is spirituality. Our point of connection to a higher power as it opens to the divine state of grace allowing inspiration to enter us. It is tied to the energy of knowing you can trust life and you are being taken care of and guided. When our crown chakra is out of balance, we can feel disconnected. Some people describe this as the dark night of the soul.

How can we tap with our Chakras?

You can do chakra tapping by incorporating the basic recipe with the EFT tapping points. However, instead of identifying the issue/challenge/ or event you would like to tap on, you would instead identify which chakra you would like to tap on. This can be chosen by allowing your intuition to guide you or perhaps going through each energy centre and doing the basic recipe on each of them.

In chakra tapping you:

1. Decide on the chakra you would like to tap on and the emotion behind it. You may write down how you feel within your body regarding this chakra.

2. Identify your SUDS. You rate it out of 10.

3. Create a set-up statement and whilst tapping on the side of the hand say the set-up statement three (3) times.

4. Tap your rounds using reminder phrases.

5. After 1-3 rounds, or where you feel is needed, check in with yourself and your rating out of 10. (SUDS)

6. Tapping on affirmations and choices you wish to ground in for a few rounds.

7. Rate the intensity again. Check SUDS again.

8. Attune to your chosen chakra for one (1) minute.

9. Seal your tapping process with a deep inhale and exhale with a sigh.

10. Allow any insights and/or reflections to arise, inviting you to write anything down if needed.

How to do the Chakra Basic Recipe

1. Decide which chakra you would like to tap on and the emotion behind it.

Once you have the chakra you would like to tap on, tune into your body. Without judgement, we want to bring in curiosity.

Now identify the emotion attached to that chakra.

Notice where you feel the emotion in your body and what those sensations feel like. Ask yourself what is beneath the emotion you are feeling?

Inviting you to close your eyes if you feel safe to do so, otherwise lower your gaze to a fixed point in front of you. Take a deep breath and check in with yourself to that chakra.

See/ hear/ feel or know if the chakra has any colour. It does not need to be a colour commonly associated with that chakra. What size is it? It does not need to be scale to the body. Does it have a shape? It doesn't need to be a spinning wheel. Texture, temperature, weight, smell and/or taste?

2. You rate the intensity – SUDS.

You rate your SUDS like you would doing the EFT Basic Recipe.

A summary identifying your SUDS is located on page 26 in this book and also on page 8 the *Foundations of*

Tapping Companion Workbook.

3. Create a Set-up statement, and whilst tapping on the side of hand, say the set-up statement three (3) times.

We begin by tapping, starting with the side of hand when we say our set-up statement before we tap on all the tapping points.

When you have chosen a set-up statement, I invite you to take a deep breath in through the nose and out through the mouth with a sigh. Allow your breathing to return to normal. Begin tapping on the side of the hand. You can use either hand. Tap with a light pressure and repeat the full set-up statement three times.

Even though... I still deeply and completely love and accept myself.

Even though I don't feel connected to my sacral chakra, I deeply and completely love and accept myself.

Even though I feel fear in my throat chakra, I deeply and completely love and accept myself.

Say the set-up statement three times whilst tapping on your side of hand (SOH). It can be the same set-up statement for all three times, or you can vary them. Allow the words to flow. There is no right or wrong.

4. Tap your rounds using reminder phrases.

As in the EFT Basic Recipe, begin a tapping round by tapping on the eyebrow point. As you tap, say out loud a part of the set-up statement, or part one of the set-up statement and information you have already obtained regarding how, what, where, when and your SUDS. Include anything you are feeling.

For tapping rounds in the chakra basic recipe, you continue to use the EFT tapping points being the eye, side of eye, under eye, under nose, chin, collar bone, underarm, and top of head points.

5. Rate the intensity again – Check your SUDS again.

After you have done a round or two, rate the intensity and your SUDS again.

Always take a moment to be in space with yourself, take in a deep breath, filling the belly with air, releasing with a sigh. Allow your body to move and stretch if it needs.

Then, rate the intensity of the emotion you are focusing on. It's normal not to feel any significant change after only one round of tapping. Keep tapping, circling back to step 4. You can start from step 3 if you prefer, and tapping for another round or two and check in to rate the intensity again. You continue this cycle until your SUDS get to a 2 or lower.

Remember you can always go back to Chapter Three in this book to refresh anything regarding going deeper through the layer.

6. Tap rounds on Affirmations and Choices.

As you tap through your rounds, however many that may be, you might be feeling a lot calmer and more relaxed. Once you have done a few rounds of tapping, even perhaps when your number is a 3 or below, begin to move into a choice and affirmation.

Below are some affirmations and choices that relate to each chakra.

Root Chakra Affirmations and Choices
- I am safe and grounded.
- I am abundant.
- I am worthy of love and care.
- I am connected to my body.
- I am filled with radiant energy.
- I am one with my true self.
- I feel peace, grounded and secure.
- I am whole and complete, exactly as I am.
- I have the courage and power to create a wonderful life.
- I trust myself, the Earth, and the universe.

Sacral Chakra Affirmations and Choices
- Creative energy flows through me.
- I enjoy pleasure in all areas of life.
- I honour the sacred body in which my soul

resides.

- I release all my emotional attachments to past feelings that no longer serve me.
- I feel powerful in embracing my sexuality.
- I breathe in powerful golden light.
- I am radiant, beautiful, creative, and enjoy a healthy and passionate life.
- I am open to the flow of creativity.
- I am safe to express myself.
- Endless prosperity flows to and through me.

Solar Plexus Chakra Affirmations and Choices

- I stand in my own personal power.
- I confidently welcome new experiences.
- I am fearless in the pursuit of what sets my soul on fire.
- I embrace my journey because it is uniquely designed for me.
- I have everything I need to create my own opportunities.
- I am free to evolve and release anything that

takes away from my growth.

- I am ready for great things with great experiences.
- I choose to prioritise myself.
- I am allowed to take up space.
- I am full of joy and happiness.

Heart Chakra Affirmations and Choices
- The power of love is inside me.
- I am ready to open up and receive love and blessings.
- I love myself and I am open to love.
- I take time to nourish my whole self.
- There is a beautiful loving light inside of me.
- Joy is the essence of my being.
- I am allowing myself to feel good.
- I give myself permission to enjoy myself.
- I step away from the prison of resentment into freedom.
- I am forgiving myself for my mistakes in my past.

Throat Chakra Affirmations and Choices
- I am a great communicator.
- I am always present when I communicate with others.
- I speak my truth freely and openly.
- I can safely communicate my feelings with others.
- I express myself with ease.
- My voice matters.
- I am allowed to be uniquely me.
- I am worthy, and who I am right now is worthy of expression.
- I expand my energy and let go of judgments.
- I show the world who I truly am.

Third Eye Chakra Affirmations and Choices
- I am wise, intuitive, and connected to my higher self.
- I am the source of my truth.
- My intuition will guide me in the right direction.

- I am open to the wisdom within.
- I am a loving soul in a human body.
- I release all blocks to my spiritual connection.
- Every day, in every way I am connecting to the universe.
- I feel love and live in peace.
- My body is a wonderful home for my beautiful soul.
- I let go of fear and I am ready to align.

Crown Chakra Affirmations and Choices

- I am worthy of love from divine energy.
- I am connected with the wisdom of the universe.
- I am open to new ideas.
- I am pure beautiful and radiant light.
- I am connected to a limitless source of creativity, abundance, health and happiness.
- I am my highest, most authentic self.
- I am aligned with my soul's purpose and truth.
- I honour the divine within me.

- I am oneness.
- I vibrate at the frequency of appreciation and joy.

PRACTICE

*Go to page 77 in the **Foundations of Tapping Companion Workbook** and list some affirmations and choices you want to include in your tapping to support your chakras.*

7. Rate the intensity again – check SUDS again.

After you have done a round or two, you will then rate the intensity and the SUDS again.

Always take a moment to be in space with yourself, take in a deep breath, fill the belly with air, and exhale with a sigh. Keep alternating between rounds 7 and 8 until you are at least a 2 or below in your SUDS.

Once you have a rating of 1 or 2, ask yourself if you still wish to hold on to this remaining number or to release it. Use your intuition. If you are asked to release it, repeat steps 7 and 8 as many times as needed until your SUD becomes a 0.

If you are happy to allow the 1 or 2 to remain, please know this is ok. Do whatever feels comfortable for you.

8. Attune to your chosen chakra for one (1) minute.

Once you have your 0 SUDS or your 1 or 2 SUD rating you are happy to keep, place your hands where you feel comfortable and attune to the chakra for one (1) minute. Allow yourself to feel the grounding and realignment within you, your nervous system, your heart, and your soul in alignment with the chakra.

9. Seal your tapping process with a deep inhale and exhale with a sigh.

Give yourself permission to inhale deeply through the nose, as your belly fills with air, and hold your breath at the top before exhaling with a sigh. Allow your body to move.

10. Insights and reflections.

Allow any insights and reflections to come through. Remind yourself it may come during or straight after your tapping, and it may even arrive sometime later.

To support your healing journey when completing the *Foundations of Tapping Companion Workbook*, a summary of the chakra basic recipe is located on page 79.

Reminders when tapping with our chakras

When we are focusing on a chakra, we are attuning to the energy within. This goes beyond the physical, beyond the 3D as we tune into the energy within our subtle body. Let your imagination help to, reconnect and strengthen your intuition.

You do not need to make this complicated. Keep it simple. Bring it back to tapping on the chakra points.

You can tap on one point, some of the points or all the points. Do what feels comfortable for you.

PRACTICE

*Use the Basic Recipe on each of your chakras in the **Foundations of Tapping Companion Workbook** from page 81. One Basic Recipe worksheet for each chakra. It may be tapping on all 7 chakras in one day, on a separate day, days in between, or something else. There is no right or wrong.*

CHAPTER SIX

Other Tapping Practices

PRACTICE

Give yourself permission to tap on the chin point for one (1) minute whilst saying,

'I release all my emotional attachments to the outdated patterns that are holding me back.'

Tapping Points for Other Tapping Practices

In EFT, you may predominantly use the face and upper body points in your tapping rounds. When using the other tapping practices described below, know you can use tapping in any way you like. You may wish to continue using the EFT tapping points rounds, you may also include finger tapping points with an EFT round and/or finger tapping rounds by themselves.

If you decide to incorporate finger-tapping rounds, remember, you can use finger-tapping using only one hand, using the fingertips to tap on the thumb point. This idea came from observing Dr. Larry Nims in his original tapping version of BSFF (Be Set Free Fast).[15] Just like EFT, you can tap on the points, rub on the points, apply slight pressure, or simply touch and/ or gently hold the tapping points.

Do what makes you feel comfortable. There is no right or wrong.

PRACTICE

Allow yourself to practice your finger tapping using only one hand. How does it feel? Do you have a specific hand you prefer to use for one hand finger tapping?

Witness Tapping

Witness Tapping allows your thoughts and feelings to come up while you tap. As you continue tapping through the points, you attune to whereabouts in your body the emotion is. This allows you to witness, validate, and acknowledge your feelings. The length of tapping is completely up to you. It is a beautiful process allowing you to feel your feelings without the need to fix, rescue, or find a solution for yourself. Remember, you are not broken. You never were. However, prior to finishing tapping, tap on any point whilst saying out loud or in your mind *'I see you.'* The words 'I see you' is you witnessing yourself. Seeing all of you without judgement.

Witness Tapping allows you the opportunity to attune to your body and is the foundation of learning before advancing into Acceptance Tapping,[16] Intention Tapping,[17] and Intuitive Intelligence Tapping[18].

PRACTICE

Find a space where you feel comfortable and tap whilst witnessing your feelings. Allow yourself to witness your feelings without the need to fix them.

PRACTICE

*Go to **Foundations of Tapping Companion Workbook** on page 96 and write down your notes and reflections on how it felt to try Witness Tapping.*

Imaginal Tapping

Imaginal tapping is where you imagine tapping on the tapping points. This is often used when you are unable to tap discreetly or if a tapping point is painful.

Imaginal tapping is also great to do if you are trying to sleep when you are tired, but your mind is active. It is also great when you want to do some tapping but may not be comfortable in an environment and/ or have the capacity to use your hands to tap.

PRACTICE

Find a space where you feel comfortable and imagine tapping on all the tapping points. Bring your intention to each tapping point and imagine you are using your fingertips to tap on each point.

PRACTICE

*Go to the **Foundations of Tapping Companion Workbook** and on page 97 write down your notes and reflections on how it felt to try Imaginal Tapping.*

Subtle Tapping

There may be times you want to tap; however, you may be in an environment where you do not want others to know. When this is the case, we use subtle tapping where we disguise that we are tapping. You could use subtle tapping when sitting at a desk where your hands are tapping on your fingers under the table. You could be in a meeting and gently tapping the gamut point.

The finger points and gamut are great for when you are in stressful meeting as you can tap them without anyone knowing.

Subtle tapping is ideal for situations where you're feeling a challenging emotion, such as sadness, frustration, rejection, anger, anxiety, or overwhelm. It's also a convenient option when you're in a place where you don't feel comfortable or don't want others to know you are tapping. Additionally, subtle tapping can be a way to take a moment for self-reflection and breathing.

PRACTICE

*Give yourself permission over the course of reading this book and the **Foundations of Tapping Companion Workbook** to bring awareness to how you may rest and/ or how you are when in a stressed state. Where are your hands resting? When you take notice of your hands being on a tapping point, allow yourself to do some tapping in whichever way feels comfortable for you on that point for one (1) minute.*

Some examples are:
- Holding your hands – Side of hand point.

- Rubbing your forehead and perhaps even eyebrows – Eyebrow point.

- Hands or fingers placed on the temples – Side of eye point.

- Elbows on the table with your chin resting in the palm of your hands. Your fingertips resting on your face – Side of eye point and under eye point.

- Hands resting around the mouth area, or perhaps even biting your nails – Under nose point and chin point.

FOUNDATIONS OF TAPPING

- Hand on your bag strap – Collar bone point.
- Arms crossed over your chest/ stomach area – Underarm point.
- Sitting back on a chair with your hands on top of your head – Top of head point.
- Fidgeting with your fingers – Fingertips points.
- Playing with a ring, especially an engagement and/ or wedding ring – Gammut Point.

PRACTICE

*Go to the **Foundations of Tapping Companion Workbook** on page 98 and write down your notes and reflections on how it felt to try Subtle Tapping.*

PRACTICE

When you are feeling sad, frustrated, rejected, anger, anxiety, overwhelm, etc, I invite you to get your SUDS (your rating out of 10) and attune to your body for how you are feeling. Practice imagining or holding each tapping point for 10-20 seconds or remain on one tapping point. Focus on how you are feeling whilst you are on each tapping point. Rate your SUDS or attune to your body again.

Continual Tapping

The amazing thing about incorporating tapping into your everyday life is you don't always have to say anything out loud, the energy from tapping alone will also benefit you. Sure, if you are doing a proper tapping round, it is best to say out loud, but know there are other ways. You don't have to tap on all the points. Try just tapping on one point. The energy from tapping on that one point alone will also benefit you.

This is where we can bring in continual tapping. We are tapping without saying anything, just toning and tuning the energy body and the nervous system. In fact, you may have done continual tapping whilst practising other tapping techniques.

You could tap when you're in the shower, waiting for the jug to boil, even while watching tv and more. You may just tap on the fingers under a table when at work for its subtlety. When we just tap, we support our body and mind to function more smoothly, raising our vibrational frequency. Steve Wells shares 'enough meridian stimulation may cause a shift in your nervous system so negative problems cannot take hold the same way.'[19]

Bring awareness to how you rest when in a stressed state. You may have your hands on your temples, hands resting under your nose, resting on your chin, crossed arms. They are all tapping points.

PRACTICE

*Go to **Foundations of Tapping Companion Workbook** on page 99 and write down your notes and reflections on how it felt to try Continual Tapping.*

Borrowed Benefits

Borrowed Benefits occur when we tap with others. You can do some tapping with your partner, tapping with your children, tapping with friends, or tapping in a group. When tapping with others, it could be all of you tapping for something relating to you, relating to them, or both.

If you are tapping with others whether it be a friend, a child, or someone else, know it can have 'borrowed benefits.' The borrowed benefits of tapping with others increase the energetic frequency. Energy increases and expands further as a collective.

PRACTICE

Invite someone to practice the tapping points with you. Bring awareness to how the energy shifts as you tap together. There may be smiles between you all, perhaps even some laughter. Feel the energy as it increases and expands. How did it feel to tap with someone else?

CHAPTER SEVEN

Inviting Tapping into Your Life

PRACTICE

Give yourself permission to tap on the collarbone point for one (1) minute whilst saying,
'I am aligning more and more with my authentic self.'

Inviting Tapping into Your Life Practices

Tapping can be easily incorporated into your everyday life and your current routine. It is beneficial to your nervous system. In this 30-Day practice you will find different ways you can incorporate tapping into your life.

You have the Basic Recipe, Personal Peace Procedure, Chakra Tapping, Witness Tapping, Continual Tapping, Subtle Tapping, Imaginal Tapping, Tapping with others allowing borrowed benefits and, in this book, you will also find some Tapping Scripts.

Some examples of inviting tapping into your life for even just a minute of your day:

- In the shower.

- Waiting for an elevator.

- Waiting for the kettle to boil.

- With my children/ partner/ friends.

- When you wake up.

- When you get into bed before I go to sleep.

- With my children before they go to bed.

- Whilst watching TV.

FOUNDATIONS OF TAPPING

- At the bus/ train/ tram/ ferry stop.
- After parking the car.
- Before/ after eating a meal.
- To replace a time where you may use your phone to scroll on social media.
- When sitting in the passenger seat of a car.
- While watching your children at sports/ creative arts training/ games/ shows.
- Waiting in line at the shops.
- During a lunch break at work.

I invite you to think of different ways you could incorporate tapping into your life. You may not do all the ways you listed in one day, especially as not every day may be the same with you and your lifestyle. For example, you may have workdays, kids sport on certain days, and more.

The ways you can bring tapping into your life could be things already mentioned in this book and its practices such as tapping in the shower, watching tv, or waiting for the kettle to boil. It could be waiting for an elevator, in your car before you get out to walk into work. It might be in a group setting like those I host on my website www.staceywebb.com.au

If you struggle to get motivated in the morning either

for work or for exercise, know you can use tapping when you wake up or before you start your day.

Tapping is great to do in the afternoon. It's nice in the afternoon when you move through that afternoon fatigue.

We may tap with our children after they've had a bad dream or when they are nervous for any reason. You can have little ones tell you about their day as you tap together.

The opportunities are endless.

PRACTICE

*Use the weekly checklist in the **Foundations of Tapping Companion Workbook** from page 102. Write down what your basic schedule is: work, kids sports days, etc., that may give you some ideas on how you can incorporate tapping into your life.*

PRACTICE

*Go to page 103 from the **Foundations of Tapping Companion Workbook** and list different ways you can bring forth a minute of tapping into your daily life.*

Aim for 30 minutes a day and break it up throughout the day to suit you. This is not a practise to overwhelm you, so please don't be focused on the time if that overwhelms your nervous system. The fact you are tapping is divine within itself.

Tapping for 30 minutes a day is a great way to bring awareness to your body with your reflections to see/hear/feel or know what emotion you feel and where in your body you feel it. Notice whether tapping is helping you feel better, especially on the days that may be more stressful. Where will you incorporate tapping into your life?

Reminders for the 30-Day Practice

One last tip I have is to let go of the need to get it right. Any recovering perfectionists out there? This isn't a right or wrong process. If you're tapping, you're doing it right. I have mentioned some different ideas and ways for you to get started, but please remember this is just one way to do this. There is no right or wrong. Once you know the basics of tapping, you can use it, however, you see fit.

Remember you're human and always tap with compassion and love for yourself. You know you're doing this work because you want to feel deep change, you want to feel happy with yourself. These are all beautiful intentions. There is nothing wrong with you if you have some habits you want to change, if you have some thoughts you'd like to shift or if you have some beliefs you'd like to release. You are a divine soul having a human experience. Let's release the pressure and always come from a place of love. Love over fear.

Tapping is a tool allowing you to voice what feels uncomfortable, allowing you to release those heavier emotions, but know outside of that, you can play with this. Tapping is amazing and I am excited to see what it can create for you. It's a really fun thing to play with.

PRACTICE

Incorporate tapping in your day, every day for 30 days using the worksheets in the ***Foundations of Tapping Companion Workbook*** *from page 106. Attached in the workbook is a daily checklist, along with both Basic Recipe worksheets and a place to write down any notes to support you.*

Chapter Eight

Tapping Scripts

PRACTICE

Give yourself permission to tap on the underarm point for one (1) minute whilst saying,
'I love who I am, who I've been and who I am becoming.'

In this chapter, there are many types of tapping scripts you can use as many times as you like. You may use some more than others. Or you may do your own tapping.

In my service as an Intuitive Trauma Release Mentor, which includes tapping, I support people on their healing journeys in a trauma informed way with the combination of intuitive intelligence and somatic embodiment tools. Therefore, within my tapping scripts in this module, you may see small parts of those other elements.

These tapping scripts are to support you and your nervous system as you work on your own healing. As such, please know these scripts are always invitational. If, for any reason, something becomes too overwhelming for your nervous system, please know you have support. You can always book in a one-on-one session with an appropriate Practitioner.

Before Each Tapping Practice

This is a practice to use before any tapping script or practice (basic recipe and/ or personal peace procedure.

Before each tapping practice, find a space you feel comfortable in to work in. You can lie down, sit, or stand. There is always the invitation to close your eyes. However, I appreciate you will be reading this, so know you can tap with your eyes open as well.

Once you have found your space, make yourself comfortable.

This may include one or more of the following:
- Moving the head in a slow motion.

- Rolling of the shoulders.

- Lifting the shoulders up towards your ears to hold before releasing them.

- Twisting the torso slowly from side to side.

- Wiggling your fingers.

- Shaking all and/ or parts of your body.

- Rubbing your hands on your thighs.

- Rubbing your hands together before placing them on your eyes, cheeks or at your nape. (Back of neck)

- Rocking on your buttocks from side to side as you sit.

- Placing your heels back.

- Wiggling your toes.

Once you have done any or all from the list above;
Bring awareness to your breath and just breathe. Breathe at your own natural timing and pace.

Letting go of all the effort it may have taken you to be here in this moment.

Giving yourself permission to be in this place.
Continuing with your awareness to your breath.
Bringing awareness to your inhale.
Bringing awareness to your exhale.

Invite your breath to start to soften. Allow a slower and deeper inhale through the nose, and exhale through either the nose or mouth. Allow all the air to release during your exhale, allowing it to be slightly longer than your inhale.

As you are breathing, place two fingers or the palm of your hand to the centre of your chest.

Allowing that touch to your heart, your heart's wisdom, and your heart's intelligence connect with your nervous system. Interconnecting to signal to the nervous system you are in a safer and braver container, right here in this space.

Continue into the tapping practice of your choice.

FOUNDATIONS OF TAPPING

Finishing Tapping Practice

This is a practice to use at the end when you have done a tapping practice, basic recipe and/ or personal peace procedure, especially if it involved moving heavy emotions.

This may include one or more of the following:

- **Move**: Move the body as it needs and shake the hands. Try for a minimum of 20 shakes.

- **Wipe**: Using the palms of your hands, wipe your hands against each other. Try for a minimum of 10 wipes.

- **Clear**: Using your thumb and index finger from one hand, wrap around the thumb on the other hand starting at the base and move in a fast motion upwards until your thumb and index finger are not touching your thumb. This is similar to pretending to take a ring off your finger. Repeat with the other fingers before repeating with the other hand.

- **Grounding**: Use the palms of your hands to press firmly down against each other.

- **Hold**: With the palms of your hands still touching each other, use your finger to hold the wrists.

- **Breathe**: Keep your hands holding each other and place them on your heart. Take a deep breath in through the nose, filling the belly with air, holding at the top until it's just past uncomfortable, and release out with a sigh.

- **Gratitude**: Say out loud or silently, 'Thank you.'

Remember the invitation is always available for you to write anything down after doing some tapping including any insights or reflections.

You can do all this practice or parts of it. There is no right or wrong. Listen to your body's wisdom and use your intuition.

Tapping and the Humming Breath

The humming breath supports you to:
- Relieve Stress.

- Invite in relaxation.

- Calm your thoughts.

- Release tension in the neck and shoulders.

It is a beautiful vibrational healing breathwork, as you can feel the vibration within your body. Vibration allows us the power to heal. We are already vibrational beings, constantly vibrating, and as we hum, we allow the vibration of our hum to essentially recalibrate within our body.

The humming also allows us to feel the vibration within our throat and is a great cleanse in clearing the energy within the throat and shoulders.

Allow yourself to do the *Before Tapping Practice* on page 109 *in this book.*

I invite you to soften your breath, inhaling through the nose and exhaling out the nose.

Inhale through the nose for 4 seconds if that feels comfortable. If you can inhale for longer, please do. And as you exhale through the nose, keep your mouth closed and hum, saying 'hmmmmmmmm' until you are out of breath.

After you have finished that hum, I invite you to tap on the side of hand as you inhale through the nose and exhale through the nose with a hum.

Tap on all the points, including your finger points repeating the process of inhaling through the nose and exhaling through the nose with a hum.

Placing your hand on your heart space, as you inhale through the nose and exhale through the nose with a hum.

Allow your breath to return to its natural rhythm and continue to feel the vibrational healing within and around you. Feel the energy as your body.

Place your hands wherever you feel comfortable and allow the body to move if it needs.

Follow the *Finishing Tapping Practice* on page 111 *in this book.*

Some questions to gain insight and reflection.

- How did the humming feel for you?

- Did the tone or strength of the hum change over time?

- Did you exhale all the way through?

- Where in your body did you feel the humming vibrations?

FOUNDATIONS OF TAPPING

Tapping for Anxiety

Follow the *Before Tapping Practice* on page 109 *in this book*.

I invite you to check in with your body to see, hear, feel, or know, how anxiety may show up within your body.

Rating the intensity from 0 – 10. 10 being the most intense.

SOH: Even though I have anxiety about (*state what it is*), I choose to feel confident and calm.

SOH: Even though I have anxiety about (*state what it is*), I allow myself to feel safe and relaxed here right now.

SOH: Even though I have anxiety about (*state what it is*), I choose to feel safe and calm.

EB: This anxiety.
SOE: This anxiety in my body.
UE: I feel this anxiety in my (*state where in the body you feel it.*)
UN: And it's a (*state your SUDS.*)
CH: I can't stop thinking about it.
CB: This anxiety.
UA: This anxiety in my body.
TOH: I feel this anxiety in my (*state where in the body you feel it.*)

EB: I feel so uncomfortable.
SOE: I wish it would go away.
UE: I feel like I am losing control.
UN: It's all too much.
CH: I'm exhausted.
CB: I don't have anything left.
UA: All this stress and anxiety I feel in my body.
TOH: This anxiety is taking over.

Place your hand on your heart, take in a deep breath, fill the belly with air, and release through the mouth with a sigh.

Just take a moment to tune into your body.

How is your body feeling? You can scan from the top of your head to the tips of your toes and see if there is any change.

What are your SUDS, rating your anxiety out of 10?

EB: I wonder what would happen if I took a moment to hear it.
SOE: To see, hear, feel, or know what my anxiety is saying.
UE: This anxiety is communicating with me.
UN: Perhaps this part of me wants to be recognised.
CH: This anxiety wants to be seen.
CB: This anxiety wants to be heard.
UA: This anxiety wants to express itself.
TOH: Instead of me wanting to run away from it.

EB: I choose not to internalise it anymore.

SOE: All this anxiety.
UE: All this fear.
UN: I choose to have fear as my ally.
CH: Instead of turning it away.
CB: This also feels uncomfortable.
UA: But I also know this is going to support me.
TOH: As I choose to have my fear as an ally.

EB: I see you.
SOE: I hear you.
UE: I feel you.
UN: I am sorry for ignoring you.
CH: I was scared of you.
CB: Maybe I don't have to be scared of fear anymore?
UA: I thank you for showing up.
TOH: I thank you for sending me messages.

EB: I choose to release all my emotional attachments to this fear.
SOE: I choose to be in the present moment.
UE: I am calm.
UN: I am relaxed.
CH: I am safe in my body.
CB: As I remember my strength and courage.
UA: It has been with me all this time.
TOH: I choose to be here.

Placing your hands on your heart space at the centre of your chest and say out loud, 'I am safe' five (5) times. Place your hand on your heart, take in a deep breath, fill the belly with air, and release through the mouth with a sigh.

Just take a moment to tune into your body.

How is your body feeling? You can scan from the top of your head to the tips of your toes and see if there is any change.

What are your SUDS, rating your anxiety out of 10?

Follow the *Finishing Tapping Practice* on page 111 *in this book.*

Please know the invitation is always here to journal after doing this tapping practice.

My Heavy Heart

Follow the *Before Tapping Practice* on page 109 *in this book.*

Rating the intensity from 0 – 10. 0 feeling congruent and safe within and 10 feeling the most disconnected or resistant.

SOH: Even though my heart feels heavy, and I don't know how much more I can take, I still deeply and completely love and accept myself *(Say three (3) times).*
EB: This feeling within my heart.
SOE: It aches.
UE: I feel uncomfortable.
UN: My heart feels heavy.
CH: I don't know how much more I can take.
CB: I can't possibly cry anymore.
UA: And yet, my heart still hurts.
TOH: Full of sadness.

EB: Full of grief.
SOE: I'm lost.
UE: I don't know who I am anymore.
UN: Will I find my way back?
CH: Can I get back?
CB: I feel stuck in this void.
UA: Blindfolded.
TOH: As I sit in darkness.

EB: In the darkness.
SOE: I feel alone.
UE: I feel empty.
UN: I feel miserable.
CH: I am full of doubts.
CB: And I don't know my way.
UA: I'm lost.
TOH: Disconnected to the world and to myself.

Place your hand on your heart space, take a deep breath, fill the belly with air, and release the exhale with a sigh.
Breathing back at your own natural rhythm.
Check in with how your body feels.
Rate the intensity, your SUDS.

EB: I choose to remember.
SOE: I choose to reconnect to my light.
UE: I choose to nurture myself with love and care.
UN: Allowing the flame to grow and expand.
CH: I choose to remember my strength and courage.
CB: I choose to remove the blindfold and step forward into my truth.
UA: I have found myself.
TOH: I have found me.

EB: I choose to give myself grace.
SOE: I choose to give myself compassion.
UE: I choose to reconnect to my wisdom.
UN: To my light.

CH: And embody my true power.
CB: I choose to allow light into my heart.
UA: As I give myself grace.
TOH: My heart feels lighter.

Place your hand on your heart space, take a deep breath, fill the belly with air, and release the exhale with a sigh.
Breathing back at your own natural rhythm.
Check in with how your body feels.
Rate the intensity, your SUDS.

SOH: It is my intention, to immerse myself with grace, compassion, and all its wisdom and love.

SOH: I release all my emotional attachments to anything and everything that may get in the way, of this happening.

SOH: I let go of all resistance I may be holding toward connecting with my light, wisdom, and love as me.

Place your hands on your heart space at the centre of your heart and say out loud, 'I love you.'
Feel, see, hear, or know your flame within growing, expanding, and shining more light within you.
Placing your hands down and, take a big inhale in through the nose, holding your breathe at the top and exhaling out through the mouth with a sigh.
Relax your hands.
And when you are ready, check in with how your body feels.

Rate your intensity, your SUDS.

Did you receive any insights or reflections?

You may wish to do the *Finishing Tapping Practice* on page 111 *in this book.*

Know you can always journal anything tapping here today and if needed, you can always do this practice again.

FOUNDATIONS OF TAPPING

Remembering My Worthiness

Follow the *Before Tapping Practice* on page 109 *in this book*.

Place two fingers or the palm of your hand to the centre of your chest, allowing them to touch your heart, your heart's wisdom, and your heart's intelligence to ignite the warmth within. See, hear, feel, or know a spark of light at the centre of your chest. You have now ignited the flame of worth within you.

Take note of how that spark is. Is it ebbing and flowing? Is it still, a large flame, a small flame or something else? Just take notice as this flame is the worthy flame within.

SOH: In the present moment. I am worthy *(Say three (3) times).*
EB: I am worthy of being here.
SOE: I am worthy of taking up space.
UE: I am worthy of existing.
UN: I am worthy of being seen.
CH: I am worthy to be alive.
CB: I am worthy of being recognised.
UA: I am worthy of moving forward.
TOH: I am worthy.

EB: I am worthy of all things wonderful.
SOE: I am worthy of love.

UE: I am worthy of healing.
UN: I am worthy of everything good in my life.
CH: I am worthy of the best things in life.
CB: I am worthy to feel the warmth.
UA: I am worthy to feel safety within.
TOH: I am worthy.

Tapping on the Heart Centre while saying:
I am worthy *(Say ten (10) times).*

Hand on your heart centre and feel the warmth of your flame within. The worthy flame you ignited at the beginning within your heart centre. See/ hear/ feel or know the warmth from the flame as it radiates throughout your whole body. Every bone, every cell.
Remembering your worth.
Relax your hands and move your body as it needs.
Allow yourself to do the *Finishing Tapping Practice* on page 111 in this book.
Continue to remember your worth. You are worthy of everything.

Believe

Allow yourself to do the *Before Tapping Practice* on page 109 *in this book.*

SOH: I choose to believe in me. All of me. Every part of me *(Say three (3) times).*
EB: I believe.
SOE: I believe in me.
UE: I believe in myself.
UN: I believe in my breath.
CH: I believe in my awareness.
CB: I believe in my expansion.
UA: I believe in my trust.
TOH: I believe in my body.

EB: I believe in my inner wisdom.
SOE: I believe in my growth.
UE: I believe in my growth.
UN: I believe in my energy.
CH: I believe in my divine self.
CB: I believe in myself.
UA: I believe in me.
TOH: I believe.

Allow yourself to be in space with this, to remember your belief in you.
Placing your hands on your heart space to anchor the

belief in yourself and embody it.

Inviting you to take a deep breath in through the nose, filling the belly with air and holding at the top until it is just past uncomfortable, before releasing out with a sigh. Allow your breath to return to its own natural rhythm.

When you are ready, allow your hands to move to a place you feel comfortable and move the body as it may need.

Allow yourself to do the *Finishing Tapping Practice* on page 111 *in this book.*

Love Tapping

Allow yourself to do the *Before Tapping Practice* on page 109 *in this book.*

EB: I am surrounded by love.
SOE: Love when I fail.
UE: Love when I rise.
UN: Love when I cry.
CH: Love when I laugh.
UA: Love.
TOH: I choose to love me.

EB: I choose to love myself.
SOE: I choose to love my reflections.
UE: I choose to love my shadows.
UN: I choose to love my light.
CH: I choose to love all of me.
UA: I choose unconditional love to my heart.
TOH: Love.
Wrist points: I choose to remind myself.
Heart Centre: That I am surrounded by love.

Placing your hands on your heart centre and see, hear, feel, or know the love that is within you.
Breathing deeply.
Knowing with every breath, the love for yourself expands effortlessly outwards until it fills your whole

body. And in your next breath the love within expands outwards surrounding your body, into your subtle body.

Allowing yourself to be filled and surrounded with your love for as much time as needed.

You may wish to do the *Finishing Tapping Practice* on page 111 *in this book.*

Root Chakra Tapping

This practice is great to use when you are feeling ungrounded, unsafe, and/ or not trusting yourself.

Allow yourself to do the *Before Tapping Practice* on page 109 *in this book.*

Bring your attention and curiosity to your root chakra as you breathe in through the nose for 4 counts and exhale through the nose or mouth for 6 counts. Continue this breath for a couple of minutes.

On a scale of 0-10, rate your intensity on connection to feeling safe, grounded, trusting with a sense of purpose. 10 being the most disconnected and 0 being feeling congruent with your root chakra.

SOH: Even though I feel ungrounded, out of balance, unstable, and unsafe, I still deeply and completely love and accept myself *(Say three (3) times).*

EB: Ungrounded.
SOE: And out of balance.
UE: Unstable.
UN: Living in fear.
CH: Unsafe.
CB: The worrying on consuming me.
UA: Feeling in secure.
TOH: Leaving me feeling unmotivated.

EB: I'm unfocused.

SOE: And feeling like I don't belong.
UE: I'm impatient.
UN: And don't feel safe within my body.
CH: I feel alone.
CB: I don't feel safe.
UA: Not fully loving myself completely.
TOH: as I don't forgive myself.

Bring your attention to your root chakra whilst saying:
Whatever is out of balance within my root chakra, I release all my emotional attachments to these feelings. I choose to bring forth safety.
Breathe in through the nose and exhale with a sigh.

EB: I choose to feel peace.
SOE: Calm.
UE: And grounded within.
UN: I am secure.
CH: I am safe.
CB: As I am loved.
UA: I love me.
TOH: I am ready.

EB: To release the heavy feelings.
SOE: I choose to release worry.
UE: And concern from within.
UN: I feel grounded.
CH: I am safe.
CB: I am secure within.

UA: As I bring forth love.
TOH: And forgiveness to myself.

Continue bringing your attention to your root chakra and see/ hear/ feel or know, a red spinning energy wheel within your root chakra. Allowing the shade of your red to expand as it spins. With every breath in and out, the red flows and blends in with your other chakras allowing the safety and trust within its grounding energy to expand and balance.

Inviting you to take a deep breath in through the nose, filling the belly with air and holding at the top before releasing out with a sigh. Allow your breath to return to its own natural rhythm.

Check in on your rating out of 10.

Allow yourself to do the *Finishing Tapping Practice* on page 111 *in this book.*

Sacral Chakra Tapping

This practice is great to use when you are feeling in denial and disappointed with life.

Allow yourself to do the *Before Tapping Practice* on page 109 *in this book.*

Bring your attention and curiosity to your sacral chakra as you breathe in through the nose for 4 counts and exhale through the nose or mouth for 6 counts. Continue this breath for a couple of minutes.

On a scale of 0-10, rate your intensity in connection to your pleasure and creativity. 10 being the most disconnected and 0 being feeling congruent with your sacral chakra.

SOH: Even though I feel a range of / or detached from my emotions as I lack pleasure and creativity within, I still deeply and completely love and accept myself *(Say three (3) times).*
EB: Unsure how to feel.
SOE: Which is detaching me from life itself.
UE: Irritable.
UN: Detaching myself.
CH: As I feel disappointed with myself.
CB: Lacking creativity from my life.
UA: Lacking pleasure from my life.
TOH: There is no flow.

EB: Comparing myself to others.
SOE: Feeling low within myself.
UE: I'm stuck.
UN: And uninspired.
CH: Feeling numb.
CB: Feeling stuck.
UA: I don't know what to do.
TOH: I don't know how to get out of this.

Bring your attention to your sacral chakra whilst saying:
Whatever is out of balance within my sacral chakra. I release all my emotional attachments to these feelings. I choose to bring forth pleasure and creativity.
Breathe in through the nose and exhale with a sigh.

EB: I am ready.
SOE: I am safe.
UE: I am free within my body.
UN: And I choose to step into my greatness.
CH: I accept myself.
CB: And see the greatness within me.
UA: Because I am pretty awesome.
TOH: Actually, I am amazing.

EB: I am powerful.
SOE: And I choose to like myself.
UE: Actually, I choose to love myself.
UN: I choose pleasure.
CH: I choose creativity.

CB: I choose passion.
UA: And I choose flow.
TOH: I choose to love myself, all of myself, just as I am.

Placing your hands on or above the sacral chakra tapping point about an inch below the navel, belly button.

Continue bringing your attention to your sacral chakra and see/ hear/ feel or know, an orange spinning energy wheel within your sacral chakra. Allowing the shade of your orange to expand as it spins. With every breath in and out, the orange flows and blends in with your other chakras allowing the creativity and pleasure within its grounding energy to expand as your sacral chakra balances within.

Inviting you to take a deep breath in through the nose, filling the belly with air and holding at the top before releasing out with a sigh. Allow your breath to return to its own natural rhythm.

Check in on your rating out of 10.

Allow yourself to do the *Finishing Tapping Practice* on page 111 *in this book.*

Solar Plexus Chakra Tapping

This practice is great to use when you are feeling low to no self-esteem and self-worth.

Allow yourself to do the *Before Tapping Practice* on page 109 *in this book.*

Bring your attention and curiosity to your solar plexus chakra as you breathe in through the nose for 4 counts and exhale through the nose or mouth for 6 counts. Continue this breath for a couple of minutes.

On a scale of 0-10, rate your intensity on connection to your self-worth, self-confidence and surrender to expand. 10 being the most disconnected and 0 being feeling congruent with your solar plexus chakra.

SOH: Even though I feel low in my self-esteem as I'm lacking confidence and don't feel good enough and I lack pleasure and creativity within, I still deeply and completely love and accept myself *(Say three (3) times).*
EB: This not feeling good enough.
SOE: This low self-esteem.
UE: This lacking confidence.
UN: Unable to take action.
CH: Wondering why even bother.
CB: I have resistance.
UA: Fearing the responsibility to take action.
TOH: Because I don't feel good enough.

EB: I don't feel worthy enough.
SOE: My will, my drive is non-existent.
UE: Fuelled with my lack of trust for myself.
UN: I don't believe in myself.
CH: What's the point?
CB: Why bother?
UA: I'm destined to be this way.
TOH: I don't feel worthy.

Bring your attention to your solar plexus chakra whilst saying:
Whatever is out of balance within my solar plexus chakra, I release all my emotional attachments to these feelings of low self-esteem and confidence. I choose to bring forth self-worth and expansion.
Breathe in through the nose and exhale with a sigh.

EB: I am ready.
SOE: I am safe.
UE: I am confident.
UN: I choose to bring forth my own personal power.
CH: I choose to bring forth my self-trust.
CB: I am motivated.
UA: I am ready.
TOH: I am powerful.

EB: I am worthy.
SOE: I am enough.
UE: Realigning and recalibrating.
UN: As I choose to reconnect to my power.

CH: I choose to reconnect to my truth.
CB: I choose to reconnect with my confidence.
UA: I can make decisions.
TOH: And will take aligned action.

Continue bringing your attention to your solar plexus chakra and see/ hear/ feel or know a yellow spinning energy wheel within your solar plexus chakra. Allowing the shade of your yellow to expand as it spins. With every breath in and out, the yellow flows and blends in with your other chakras allowing your self-worth and expansion within its grounding energy to expand as your solar plexus chakra balances within.

Inviting you to take a deep breath in through the nose, filling the belly with air and holding at the top before releasing out with a sigh. Allow your breath to return to its own natural rhythm.

Check in on your rating out of 10.

Allow yourself to do the *Finishing Tapping Practice* on page 111 *in this book.*

Heart Chakra Tapping

This practice is great to use when you are feeling abandoned, jealous, and rejected by life.

Allow yourself to do the *Before Tapping Practice* on page 109 *in this book.*

Bring your attention and curiosity to your heart chakra as you breathe in through the nose for 4 counts and exhale through the nose or mouth for 6 counts. Continue this breath for a couple of minutes.

On a scale of 0-10, rate your intensity regarding your acceptance, forgiveness, wholeness, and compassion. 10 being the most disconnected and 0 being feeling congruent with your heart chakra.

SOH: Even though I feel scared of opening myself up to love, I'm worried I'll get hurt. This leaves me feeling lonely, not providing myself love as well, I still deeply and completely love and accept myself *(Say three (3) times).*

EB: I'm scared to love.
SOE: And open up.
UE: Scared to be loved.
UN: And be intimate.
CH: I don't want to get hurt.
CB: And yet I feel alone and isolated.
UA: I'm closing myself off from the world.
TOH: Holding in judgement.

EB: Judgement to others and myself.
SOE: Not loving myself as a whole.
UE: Not upholding boundaries to myself and others.
UN: Deep down I'm unforgiving.
CH: Lacking self-compassion.
CB: As I close myself off to the world.
UA: Believing it's better this way.
TOH: Holding myself back from life.

Bring your attention to your heart chakra whilst saying:
Whatever is out of balance within my heart chakra, I release all my emotional attachments to these feelings. I choose to bring forgiveness, acceptance, wholeness, and compassion.
Breathe in through the nose and exhale with a sigh.

EB: I am ready.
SOE: I am safe.
UE: I call in love.
UN: Kindness and generosity.
CH: Opening my heart to the world.
CB: Allowing the giving and receiving of love.
UA: I give myself permission to receive support.
TOH: I return and reconnect to my heart centre.

EB: To know I am love itself.
SOE: And always connected to love.
UE: Realigning and recalibrating.

UN: As I choose to reconnect to my power.
CH: I choose to bring forth forgiveness.
CB: I choose to bring forth acceptance.
UA: I choose to bring forth self-compassion.
TOH: I choose wholeness.

Continue bringing your attention to your heart chakra and see/ hear/feel or know a green spinning energy wheel within your heart chakra. Allowing the shade of your green to expand as it spins. With every breath in and out, the green flows and blends in with your other chakras allowing the forgiveness, acceptance, wholeness, and compassion within its grounding energy to expand as your heart chakra balances within.

Inviting you to take a deep breath in through the nose, filling the belly with air and holding at the top before releasing out with a sigh. Allow your breath to return to its own natural rhythm.

Check in on your rating out of 10.

Allow yourself to do the *Finishing Tapping Practice* on page 111 *in this book.*

Throat Chakra Tapping

This practice is great to use when you are afraid to speak or to be seen and maybe living life out of fear.

Allow yourself to do the *Before Tapping Practice* on page 109 *in this book.*

Bring your attention and curiosity to your throat chakra as you breathe in through the nose for 4 counts and exhale through the nose or mouth for 6 counts. Continue this breath for a couple of minutes.

On a scale of 0-10, rate your intensity on connection to speaking your voice, your truth, to being seen and not living in fear, and whether you are living out of love or fear. 10 being the most disconnected and 0 being feeling congruent with your throat chakra.

SOH: Even though I feel scared to speak my truth, to voice my feelings, leaving unable to express myself, I still deeply and completely love and accept myself *(Say three (3) times).*

EB: Scared to speak my truth.
SOE: Scared to voice my feelings.
UE: My voice is small and doesn't count.
UN: Leaving me unable to express myself.
CH: As I suppress my feelings.
CB: I am frustrated.
UA: I don't want to be hurt or judged.
TOH: I don't want to hurt others.

EB: Maybe I should just stay quiet?
SOE: But I'm not honouring my voice.
UE: Scared to share parts of me.
UN: Scared to reveal the real me.
CH: In fear.
CB: I will be rejected by others.
UA: And as a result, I am rejected.
TOH: My true self.

Bring your attention to your throat chakra whilst saying:
Whatever is out of balance within my throat chakra, I release all my emotional attachments to these feelings. I choose to bring open and honest communication, the expression of my truth.

Breathe in through the nose and exhale with a sigh.

EB: I am ready.
SOE: I am safe.
UE: I choose to make space for me.
UN: My truth deserves to be heard.
CH: I choose to bring forth confidence.
CB: As I feel empowered.
UA: I choose to bring forth openness and honesty to myself.
TOH: I choose to communicate with myself and others.

EB: I choose to express my truth.

SOE: I choose to express me.
UE: Realigning and recalibrating.
UN: I am enough.
CH: I choose to reconnect to my truth.
CB: I choose to reconnect with my self-trust.
UA: I choose to reconnect back to my authenticity.
TOH: Allowing myself to be seen and heard.

Continue bringing your attention to your throat chakra and see/ hear/ feel or know a blue spinning energy wheel within your throat chakra. Allowing the shade of your blue to expand as it spins. With every breath in and out, the blue flows and blends in with your other chakras allowing the open, honest communication as you express your truth within its grounding energy to expand as your blue chakra balances within.

Inviting you to take a deep breath in through the nose, filling the belly with air and holding at the top before releasing out with a sigh. Allow your breath to return to its own natural rhythm.

Check in on your rating out of 10.

Allow yourself to do the *Finishing Tapping Practice* on page 111 *in this book.*

Third Eye Chakra Tapping

This practice is great to use when you are feeling disconnected from yourself, your light, intuition, and your spirituality.

Allow yourself to do the *Before Tapping Practice* on page 109 *in this book.*

Bring your attention and curiosity to your third eye chakra as you breathe in through the nose for 4 counts and exhale through the nose or mouth for 6 counts. Continue this breath for a couple of minutes.

On a scale of 0-10, rate your intensity on connection to light, your intuition and spirituality. 10 being the most disconnected and 0 being feeling congruent with your third eye chakra.

SOH: Even though I feel stuck in my daily routine, stagnant and unable to establish a proper vision for myself as I lack clarity and focus, I still deeply and completely love and accept myself *(Say three (3) times).*
EB: Feeling stuck.
SOE: Feeling stagnant.
UE: Indecisive.
UN: Unable to establish a proper routine.
CH: Lacking clarity and focus.
CB: Disconnected to my imagination.
UA: Disconnected and not trusting of my intuition.
TOH: I can't see vision and purpose.

EB: My imagination and creativity are stagnant.
SOE: I can't move forward or set goals.
UE: In denial and in tunnel vision.
UN: Feeling stuck.
CH: And disconnected from my path.
CB: Not trusting my intuition.
UA: Lacking my awareness.
TOH: I don't believe in myself.

Bring your attention to your third eye chakra whilst saying:
Whatever is out of balance within my third eye chakra, I release all my emotional attachments to these feelings. I choose to bring forth awareness, to listen and follow my intuition.

Breathe in through the nose and exhale with a sigh.

EB: I am ready.
SOE: I am safe.
UE: I choose clarity.
UN: And I choose to harness my vision.
CH: I choose to bring forth my self-trust.
CB: I choose to reconnect to my awareness.
UA: I choose to reconnect to my intuition.
TOH: As I reconnect with life.

EB: I choose to come back to my centre.
SOE: To my imagination and intuition.
UE: Realigning to my highest frequency.

UN: As I choose to reconnect with my inner knowing.
CH: Trusting and following my intuition.
CB: Trusting my creativity.
UA: With clear direction.
TOH: To move forward with my focus.

Continue bringing your attention to your third eye chakra and see/ hear/ feel or know an indigo spinning energy wheel within your third eye chakra. Allowing the shade of your indigo to expand as it spins. With every breath in and out, the indigo flows and blends in with your other chakras allowing your awareness to listen and follow your intuition within its grounding energy to expand as your crown chakra balances within.

Inviting you to take a deep breath in through the nose, filling the belly with air before releasing out with a sigh. Allow your breath to return to its own natural rhythm.

Check in on your rating out of 10.

Allow yourself to do the *Finishing Tapping Practice* on page 111 *in this book.*

Crown Chakra Tapping

This practice is great to use when you are feeling disconnected with yourself, your identity and living in fear.

Allow yourself to do the Before Tapping Practice on page 109 *in this book.*

Bring your attention and curiosity to your crown chakra as you breathe in through the nose for 4 counts and exhale through the nose or mouth for 6 counts. Continue this breath for a couple of minutes.

On a scale of 0-10, rate your intensity on connection to self, your higher self, and whether you are living out of love or fear. 10 being the most disconnected and 0 being feeling congruent with your crown chakra.

SOH: Even though I feel separated and disconnected from myself, my higher self, and life itself. Lacking faith and struggling, lost, and confused, I still deeply and completely love and accept myself *(Say three (3) times).*

EB: I feel disconnected.
SOE: Lonely and isolated.
UE: My faith and trust in the divine has short circuited.
UN: I'm lost, confused, and struggling with life.
CH: Wondering what I'm doing here and purpose in life.
CB: Lacking direction.
UA: Unable to move forward.

TOH: In faith trust and flow.

EB: I don't know who I am.
SOE: I have no identity.
UE: Who am I?
UN: I don't know anymore.
CH: I don't trust in myself anymore.
CB: Why bother?
UA: I don't even know who I am.
TOH: As I am disconnected to myself, my higher self and to life itself.

Bring your attention to your crown chakra whilst saying:
Whatever is out of balance within my crown chakra, I release all my emotional attachments to these feelings. I choose to reconnect back to my higher power and trust life itself.
Breathe in through the nose and exhale with a sigh.

EB: I am ready.
SOE: I am safe.
UE: I choose to be connected to myself, my higher self and life.
UN: And I choose to bring forth my own personal power.
CH: I choose connection.
CB: I choose trust.
UA: I am not alone.
TOH: Love is always available to me.

EB: Love is always available to all parts of me.
SOE: I trust myself.
UE: Realigning and reconnecting.
UN: To my higher self.
CH: And to my faith in believing in myself.
CB: I surrender in the unknown.
UA: As my path unfolds.
TOH: I am divinely connected.

Continue bringing your attention to your crown chakra and see/ hear/ feel or know a violet or white spinning energy wheel within your crown chakra. Allowing the shade of your violet or white to expand as it spins. With every breath in and out, the violet or white flows and blends in with your other chakras allowing the creativity and pleasure within its grounding energy to expand as your crown chakra balances within.

Inviting you to take a deep breath in through the nose, filling the belly with air and holding at the top before releasing out with a sigh. Allow your breath to return to its own natural rhythm.

Check in on your rating out of 10.

Allow yourself to do the *Finishing Tapping Practice* on page 111 *in this book.*

PRACTICE

Go to page 228 in **Foundations of Tapping Companion Workbook** *and write your own tapping practices.*

CHAPTER NINE

Reflection

PRACTICE

Give yourself permission to tap on the top of head point for one (1) minute whilst saying,
'I release all my emotional attachments to who I have been told to see myself as. I accept myself for who I am.'

Throughout this book, we have gone on a journey where you have invited EFT and other tapping practices into your life through the foundations of EFT.

Now is the time to reflect on your journey.

PRACTICE

*Go to page 234 of the **Foundations of Tapping Companion Workbook** and answer the reflection questions.*

1. Church, D., Stapleton, P., Vasudevan, A., & O'Keefe, T. (2022) Clinical EFT as an evidence-based practice for the treatment of psychological and physiological conditions: A systematic review.
2. Van der Kolk, B. A. (2014). The body keeps the score: Brain, mind, and body in the healing of trauma.
3. Ortner, N. (2015) 4th Australian edition. The Tapping Solution. A revolutionary system for stress-free living. McPherson's Printing Group Australia p5.
4. https://www.emofree.com/fr/eft-tutorial/tapping-basics/what-is-eft.html
5. Bach, D., Groesbeck, G., Stapleton, P., Banton, S., Bickheuser, K., & Church, D. (2018) Journal of Evidence Based Integrative Medicine © Mind Heart Connect 2018.
6. https://englishstudyhere.com/vocabulary/list-of-emotions/
7. https://patcarrington.com/introducing-the-choices-method/
8. https://blog.trello.com/limiting-beliefs
9. https://theworl.com/instruction-the-work-byron-katie/
10. https://tappingqanda.com/2010/07/psychological-reversal-2/
11. https://www.emofree.com/articles-ideas/general-ideas/secondary-gains-stewart-articles.html

12. Ortner, N. (2015) 4th Australian edition. The Tapping Solution. A revolutionary system for stress-free living. McPherson's Printing Group Australia p24.
13. https://www.youtube.com/watch?v=br8-qebjIgs
14. https://eftuniverse.com/refinements-to-eft/the-generalization-effect/
15. https://www.besetfreefast.com/what-is-be-set-free-fast
16. https://intentionaltapping.com/tapping/
17. https://intentiontapping.com/tapping/
18. https://instituteforintuitiveintelligence.com/
19. https://www.eftdownunder.com/

Thank You

Thank you for allowing me to be a part of your support system. This book, along with the *Foundations of Tapping Companion Workbook* was designed to support you in your healing journey and I hope it has supported you. Healing journeys are cyclical in nature, so please know you can always come back to this book and the *Foundations of Tapping Companion Workbook*.

There are many layers within the tapping world. This book has demonstrated the foundations of EFT and other tapping practices.

Tapping is a great tool to do by yourself and I hope by reading and participating in the practises you could incorporate tapping into your life. Although tapping can be done by yourself, it doesn't mean you must only do it by yourself. If anything is overwhelming your system, know you can have extra support and guidance with an appropriate Practitioner.

Embarking on our healing journey is a journey in discovering yourself. Know that tapping can be a part of your support system.

All my love, Stacey

Resources

If you would like to read and study more on what is presented within this workbook, please feel free to look at these resources.

Angelique Adams, Intuitive Intelligence Tapping, https://instituteforintuitiveintelligence.com/

Brad Yates, https://www.tapwithbrad.com/

Dawson Church, https://www.dawsonchurch.com

Embrace Empowerment, EFT Practitioner certification, https://www.embraceempowerment.com

Gary Craig, https://www.emofree.com/

Gene Monterastelli, https://tappingqanda.com/

Intention Tapping, https://intentiontapping.com/

Patricia Carrington, https://www.patcarrington.com

Peta Stapleton, https://www.petastapleton.com/

Stacey Webb, https://www.staceywebb.com.au

Steve Wells, https://stevewells.com.au/

The Tapping Solution, https://www.thetappingsolution.com/

Letter of Gratitude

It is with the deepest gratitude I acknowledge the extraordinary people who supported the birth of my book into the world.

Thank you to my husband Grant. I am forever grateful for your love and support in standing by my side and making sacrifices to help bring this book to the world. You and our four children, Vanessa, Rhiannon, Ashton, and Adeline make my heart sing.

To Karen McDermott. Thank you for mentoring, supporting, and guiding me to publish this book. I cherish our friendship. You are an angel.

To my editor Dannielle Line, illustrator Rachael Cannard, and book designer Ida Jansson, thank you for supporting me and my vision for birthing this book into the world.

Thank you to my teachers both formal and informal. Tapping has saved me and for that, I am forever grateful. Particularly thank you to my Intuitive Intelligence Tapping Teacher, Angelique Adams, and EFT Teacher, Kadine Aharon. You both have taught, supported, and guided me to be the leader I am today. I love you both so much. Special mention to Alison Haitana, Kia West, Colleen Bloomfield, Lisa Benson, and Louise O'Reilly for your continued love.

To my circle of heart-centered humans who provide unconditional support to me. You know who you are. I am grateful for our friendship and love you all so much.

Thank you to you, dear reader. I honour you for wanting to use tapping practices to support your healing journey and I feel privileged you have used my book to be a part of your journey.

I see you.
I honour you.
I love you.

About the Author

Stacey Webb is an award-winning author, Intuitive Somatic Mentor, Trauma-Trained Somatic Practitioner, and Warrior of Grace who resides in Australia with her husband and four children.

During her 16-year career as a detective within the police force, Stacey has studied trauma, the nervous system, and has obtained many certifications and qualifications in EFT, breathwork, somatic therapy, embodiment, and intuitive intelligence. This is to support people on their healing journey as they; release trauma, stored emotions, energy blocks and limiting beliefs that may be creating limitations.

Stacey is also the author of 'The Intuitive Detective' which has received amazing reviews from readers all over the world including winning multiple book awards.

Where to find me

Before you close this book, I would love to remind you that I am a real person who genuinely wants to support people on their healing journey. If you would like to work with me, or just want to get in touch, you can contact me through my website or on social media.

Website: www.staceywebb.com.au

f
facebook.com/StaceyWebbEFT

instagram.com/_staceywebb

amazon.com/author/staceywebb

g
goodreads.com/author/show/22384693.Stacey_Webb

tiktok.com/@_staceywebb

▶
youtube.com/@Staceywebb

www.ingramcontent.com/pod-product-compliance
Lightning Source LLC
Chambersburg PA
CBHW050313010526
44107CB00055B/2229